STANDING AGAINST THE RAGE

STANDING AGAINST THE RAGE

*Based on the true story of Mildred Flatau's miraculous escape
from domestic violence.*

By Linda D'Ae-Smith

Published 2020 by Shorehouse Books

Printed in the United States of America

ISBN-13: 978-0-9600085-8-2

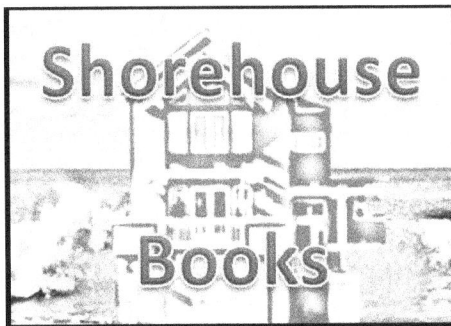

DEDICATION

This book is dedicated to the life and memory of Mildred Elisabeth Flatau Cape. She serves as an inspiration for overcoming and thriving in spite of incredible tragedy and loss.

ACKNOWLEDGMENTS

Thank you to the following:

Sandy Historical Society, Sandy, Oregon
Oregon City Historical Society, Oregon City, Oregon
Malheur County Historical Society, Ontario, Oregon
Bannock County Historical Society, Pocatello, Idaho
Detroit Historical Society, Detroit, Michigan
Immanuel Lutheran Church, Sandy, Oregon
Grace Community Church, Detroit, Michigan

Caroline Koivisto, Grace Wewer Reich, and Viola Wunische Stirdivant
Gale and Sharon Meier
Charles and Laura Herrell
Rebecca Koepke Arnold
Carolyn Bohan

The late Lake Bogan

The National Domestic Violence Hotline

This book would not have been possible without the cooperation of Mildred's family: Danell Cape Rutherford, Evelyn Buckstein Morgan, and Donald Steinhart. Their stories, historical documents, letters, and photos are invaluable.

Finally, a huge thank you to my husband, Christopher Smith. His loving encouragement keeps my fingers on the keyboard.

.

About the Author

Linda (Detherage) D'Ae-Smith is a native of Oregon and has lived the majority of her life in the Sandy area.

She and her husband Christopher both graduated from Sandy High School, but didn't begin dating until Chris started attending Linda's church. They were married June 16, 1979, and have two adult children. One of the greatest joys of their life is their three granddaughters.

Throughout elementary and high school, Linda enjoyed writing and focused on creative writing and public relations in college. Her love of writing led to a job in public/media relations at Oregon Zoo from 1996 – 2011, writing press releases for local, national, and international distribution, as well as magazine articles for The Association of Zoo and Aquarium's magazine, *Connect*.

Linda and Christopher enjoy their home and spending time in Central Oregon, as well as traveling to national parks. They have a goal of visiting all sixty-two parks.

Linda's blog can be found at www.femme-de-finesse.com

INTRODUCTION - MY PERSONAL JOURNEY

There's not a better place on the planet than my backyard patio on a summer afternoon. The skies are a brilliant blue with wispy white clouds and the warmth of the sun is rarely intense. The sounds of the water cascading over the rocks in our nearby water feature accompany the birds as they cheerily splash and then flit from tree to tree. I'm mesmerized by the soaring red-tailed hawks that visit our freshly mowed fields looking for a tasty meal. They glide along effortlessly, or so it seems.

My husband grew up on this forty-acre plot of land that we share with his family. I've heard stories from his childhood many times over, although a new one surfaces from time to time. My adult children now tell stories of their escapades on the property with their cousins, some which were downright dangerous.

This property is rich with family memories for three, and now four generations, but the history of the property also includes a dark episode that pre-dates family ownership. It's an episode that my husband's family discovered after purchasing the property.

I don't recall the first time I heard the "Legend of Flatau" (as my husband used to call it), but it must have been shortly after we started dating in 1977. The home, barn, and outbuildings that the previous owner Edward Flatau built are long gone. The house was destroyed before my husband's family purchased the property, but we stored hay in the old barn until the mid-80s. My husband used the old outbuildings to raise hogs when he was a member of Future

Farmers of America in high school. They were removed to make way for construction of our home. The only visual reminder of the Flatau farm is the hand-dug well, which was declared unsanitary and has been capped for nearly ninety years. I can see it from my kitchen window.

Photo of the old barn built by Edward Flatau and his hired hand,
Paul Buuck. It was used by the Smith family until the mid-80s.
Photo courtesy of Ruth Smith.

While the tangible reminders of the family are mostly gone, the story of Edward, Anna, Frances, Mildred, and Mabel Flatau is unforgettable. In particular, Mildred's part of the story is so compelling that I knew it must be told. Her strength in the midst of horrific tragedy is, on the surface, inexplicable. What causes a young teen to stand up against the rage of a man seeking vengeance upon perceived injustice? I was driven to find the answer, and set out on a remarkable journey to uncover Mildred's story.

When my husband worked for *The Oregonian* newspaper he mentioned the incident to a co-worker who proceeded to get copies of the story that ran in the newspaper regarding the episode. This provided great background material, but I really wanted to talk to relatives of Mildred and Frances. The newspaper story indicated they were teenagers in 1933, so I assumed both Mildred and Frances had died.

I knew they had visited the property in 1983, which would have been the 50th anniversary of the incident. My father-in-law had even had a conversation with them, but he had passed away in 2007, and it's doubtful he would have remembered much of the conversation. I had no idea where they had moved after the incident, so I really didn't even know where to start looking.

I've had pretty good luck tracking down my relatives using Ancestry.com, so I thought maybe I'd try to contact Mildred's relatives in the same manner. I wasn't successful until I included the very blurry photos from the newspaper article. A day or two after the photos had been added, Mildred's great-nephew contacted me. He graciously put me in touch with his mother Evelyn, and she introduced me to Mildred's daughter Danell. Both Evelyn and Danell have been very supportive and provided me with resource material including Mildred's official statement to the police as well as the diary she kept as she traveled from Oregon to Michigan with her Uncle August and Aunt Elisabeth. Evelyn's son has been helpful with scanning the family photos included in this book.

Both Danell and Evelyn had been kept in the dark regarding the circumstances of their maternal grandparents' deaths, so they felt I could benefit from speaking to their mother's old school friend, Alvina. They didn't know if she was still living, but thought it might be worth the effort to try to track her down. They had her married name from a second marriage, which yielded no results. After more digging, they were able to provide her last name from a first marriage. Unfortunately that information revealed that she too had passed away. However, it also revealed her maiden name, and I was absolutely floored when I immediately recognized it as the family name of some longtime friends of our family.

I called the family friend, who confirmed that Alvina was her aunt. She also shared that her Aunt Viola, Alvina's last surviving sibling, was coming to visit in a few weeks. Viola was in her nineties, but had a good recollection of the past. She also suggested that I meet Grace, a longtime resident of Sandy who probably remembered the incident.

I met with these two elderly ladies, and was shocked to learn that Grace was the granddaughter of Edward Flatau's cousin Ida Miller. Ida and her husband Herman were also neighbors of the Flataus. In addition, Grace was familiar with the history of the Immanuel Lutheran Church in Sandy where the Flatau family had attended services.

It has been an interesting journey, and with each step, I have felt God was telling me to write this book. Everything I have needed, from historical information to family records, has fallen into my lap. I am grateful to have been entrusted with the telling of Mildred's story.

Chapter One
Mildred's Journey Begins, Tuesday, April 11, 1933

Mildred stood in the drizzling rain and bowed her head to pray. "Be mindful, O Lord, of Mother and Mabel and all who have fallen asleep in the hope of the resurrection unto eternal life. Shelter them in a place of brightness."

She stopped, unable to continue the prayer. The words were stuck in her throat. Somehow God would understand. He knew what she'd been through. Did she need to pray at all, she wondered. No one could tell her God was not with her that awful day. He was there and He knew.

Mildred swallowed hard, silently looking at the only earthly reminder of her mother Anna and her sister Mabel. Their fresh graves were all that remained other than memories. Some memories she worked hard to imprint on her heart so she would never forget. Others she wished she could erase like chalk from a blackboard. If she could, she'd wipe out every memory of March 17.

Looking down the row of neatly tended graves, Mildred noticed the headstones and markers. She hoped that one day a beautiful headstone would mark the graves of her mother and sister. Her older sister Frances had been able to purchase the two plots for $74 financed over the next six months. The payment for just the plots was going to be difficult for Frances to afford. Headstones were out of the question. This would have to do for now. At least he wasn't buried next to them. At least he was far away in another cemetery in another town.

Her Uncle August and Aunt Elisabeth stood quietly behind her, patiently waiting for her to say her final goodbye. They had a long road trip ahead and were anxious to get underway, but understood it would be a long time, if ever, before Mildred would return to Oregon once she was settled in their home in Michigan. They backed away from Mildred, sensing she needed to be alone.

Mildred knew it was time to go. Rose City Cemetery was their final stop before leaving everything she'd ever known. Aunt Elisabeth had packed food for lunch, the car had been filled with gasoline, they'd said goodbye to Frances, and now she just needed to walk back to the car before the tears began to fall from her blue eyes. She didn't cry the day her world collapsed. She hadn't cried and she wouldn't.

Mildred breathed in deeply, feeling the damp, cool air fill her lungs. "Goodbye, Mother….goodbye, Mabel," Mildred whispered as she turned to walk to the car. "Goodbye…"

She wished she could stay with Frances, who had been working in Portland since graduating high school nearly a year ago. After all, Mildred's sixteenth birthday was a week ago and Frances would be twenty in the fall. They were both practically grown women, thought Mildred, which made it difficult to understand why Frances had agreed that it would be better for her to move to Detroit and settle into a new home with Uncle August and Aunt Elisabeth. Frances assured her she would visit her in Detroit, just as soon as the details of the estate were settled and the farm was sold.

Oh, how she wished she were back on the farm in Sandy with Mother, Frances, and Mabel, but not him. No, not him!

Mildred opened the car door and slid into the back seat. She brushed her damp, blond hair away from her face. She briefly glanced toward Uncle August and Aunt Elisabeth, two people she barely knew, before turning her face toward the car window. Rain streamed down the glass like tears flowing uncontrollably. Mildred sat rigid with her hands clasped firmly in her lap. Everyone was quiet as they drove slowly and respectfully through the cemetery. Mildred pulled her grey winter coat more tightly around her. She thought it strange that she felt the chill more in the car than she had as she stood outside by the graves.

Uncle August pulled the car onto the road and headed toward the Columbia River Highway. As they traveled through the steady rain, the rhythmic swish of the car's windshield wipers lulled Mildred into deep thought.

Friday, March 17, 1933
Sandy Ridge – 7:30 a.m.

Mildred heard her mother's firm voice and stirred under the warmth of thick blankets. She wanted to stay in bed, but that wasn't an option. She stretched a bit before sitting up and swinging her legs out from under the covers. Pulling open the dresser drawer, she spied one of Frances' old dresses that had been handed down to her. It had been a little big for her the last time she tried it on, but thought it might be just right now.

It was a cheery print of pink nosegays on a cream-colored background; perfect for spring. Mildred slipped the dress over her head and was pleased at how it fit. Every time she'd seen Frances wear this dress, she was a bit envious. It was by far her favorite of the recent set of hand-me-down clothing.

"Come on, Mabel," she said as she pulled on her long knit stockings. "It's time to get up and get ready for school."

"It's too cold," whined Mabel.

"You'll warm up. Come on, Mabel. You don't want Mother to call us again."

Mabel crawled out of the bed she shared with Mildred and ran to the dresser to get her clothes, chattering her teeth dramatically.

"It's not that cold, Mabel," said Mildred rolling her eyes. "I'm going downstairs to help Mother with breakfast." Mildred walked over to Mabel and whispered in her ear, "Hurry so we can leave for school before anything happens."

Mabel nodded her head as Mildred headed for the stairs.

Descending the steep, narrow, creaky staircase, Mildred caught a whiff of the oatmeal cooking on the stove mixed with the scent of freshly brewed coffee. She uttered a cursory, "Good morning," to no one in particular.

As she entered the tiny kitchen, Mildred noticed her father at the table drinking a cup of coffee. He looked in her direction, acknowledging her presence, but said nothing. Her eyes averted his glance. She looked out the window toward the back field. It was almost spring and the bare landscape around the Flatau farm in Sandy was beginning to show the signs of new life. Wildflowers were starting to pop up through the hard soil, the field grass was growing and the maple trees were beginning to bud. The seasons were changing, but not even the warmth of spring could thaw the icy cold relationship between her mother and father.

"Take these bowls to the table, Mildred," Mother said without turning from the stove.

Mildred was placing the two bowls of hot oatmeal on the table as Mabel entered the kitchen and stood next to the stove shifting her weight from foot to foot in an effort to get warm. Their father looked over at Mabel and shook his head at the theatrics, but Mildred noticed a slight grin pass his lips. Both girls stood behind their chairs and prayed. "Come Lord Jesus, be our guest and let these gifts to us be blessed. Amen."

Mildred and Mabel sat down and ate their breakfast quickly and quietly. Even though their parents hadn't uttered a word to one another, the tension building between them was palpable. It was like a thick, dark cloud bank enveloping the entire house.

Mildred's mother Anna began to speak with her back turned away from the table where her daughters and husband sat. "Edward, you know we need the milk separator to make sour cream.

You know we need to make sour cream to make money. You must move the milk separator to the milk house today!"

Edward became instantly angry and slammed his coffee cup against the table, causing Mildred and Mabel to jump. "You think it's my fault that our milk was degraded. You blame me, don't you?"

Anna turned around to face her husband. "I blame you for not moving the milk separator to the milk house so we can make sour cream from the degraded milk," she retorted. "It is your fault we aren't making any money."

Every morning for the last few weeks, the conversation was the same, thought Mildred. Her mother reminded her father daily about the need for the milk separator. Mildred didn't understand why her father procrastinated in moving the separator from the outbuilding to the milk house, but it wasn't unusual for him to be obstinate, especially with requests made by her mother. This wasn't the first time this obstinacy had caused an argument between her parents. No wonder her older sister Frances had been anxious to take a job as a maid in Portland right after graduating high school.

Anna continued to reprimand Edward for his negligence. "It's your responsibility to put food on this table for your family!"

"Why did I marry you? Twenty years of marriage and not one day of happiness," asked Edward rhetorically.

"Almost twenty-three years," corrected Anna.

"It seems longer," replied Edward. "Every day you do nothing but nag. Everyday it's the same. Nothing is good enough for you!"

Edward's rant continued, interspersed with cursing and calling Anna names that made Mildred and Mabel cringe. Anna countered with angry words of her own.

Mildred's appetite was gone, but she continued to eat her oatmeal. She noticed Mabel swinging her legs under the table and humming a song to herself to shut out the noise. Mildred wished she could tune out the arguing, as well.

Uncle August and Aunt Elisabeth noticed the quietness that had settled over Mildred.

"Why don't we stop at Multnomah Falls?" suggested Aunt Elisabeth.

"Oh, yes, please," responded Mildred. She was relieved to be distracted from the unpleasant memories, and who knew when she'd have the opportunity to see the magnificent falls again. Even in the rain, the falls were spectacular.

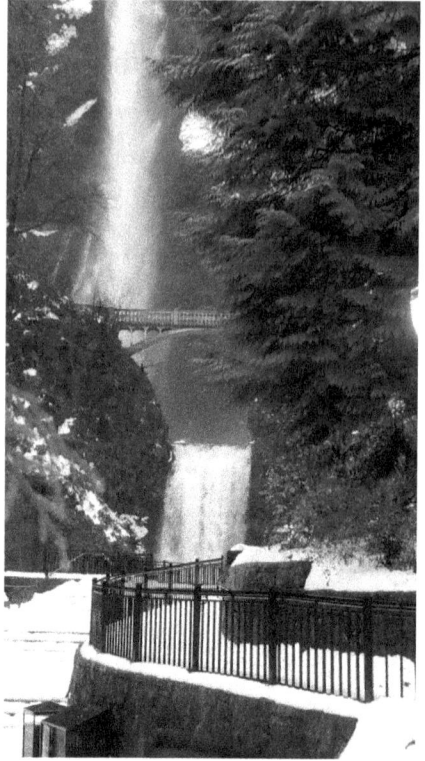

Multnomah Falls in autumn and winter (present day).
Photos courtesy of Renee Detherage.

They parked the car and walked to the lower viewing area. Towering Douglas fir trees framed the magnificent falls. The beauty of the water as it fell from more than 600 feet above was an image Mildred wanted to preserve in her memory. She closed her eyes and listened to the rushing of the water. If only it would wash away those memories. It was a strong and powerful sound, yet strangely soothing. For the first time in a long time Mildred felt a sense of peace and prayed silently.

"Our Father who art in heaven, hallowed be thy name. Thy kingdom come, thy will be done on earth as it is in heaven."

She opened her eyes and saw Uncle August and Aunt Elisabeth looking at her. Suddenly self-conscious, she smiled and turned her eyes back to the falls. Everyone was awkwardly quiet.

After a few minutes, Aunt Elisabeth broke the silence. "We should get back on the road, August. We want to get to Ontario[*] before it gets too late."

Mildred wasn't ready to leave, but she obediently followed her Aunt and Uncle back to the car. Not wishing to relive the nightmare of her parent's argument, she got out paper and pencil to write about her trip in a letter to Frances.

Dear Frances,

After leaving Portland, we drove east on the Columbia River Highway and stopped at Multnomah Falls. Remember when we went there and how magnificent it was? We didn't

---

[*] Founded in 1883, Ontario, Oregon, was named after Ontario, Canada. It is the largest city in Malheur County with a population of just over 11,000 and is located along the Snake River at the Idaho border. The population when Mildred spent the night there was less than 2000, but that would have seemed relatively large compared to her hometown of Sandy with a population of less than 300.

stay long, because we want to reach Ontario to spend the night.

About ten minutes after we left the falls, we saw an accident that appeared to have happened last night. A truck hauling wood had run into the fence and upset its load. It was sure a mess, but we didn't stop.

It was fun going through the tunnels! It's been so long since I've gone through a tunnel that it was almost like I was experiencing something new!

It finally stopped raining when we got to Hood River, and when we got to the viewpoint, Uncle August stopped and let us look around. We looked across the Columbia River and around at the mountains.

We drove on to The Dalles. That's where the prairie begins. We followed the Columbia River until we reached Umatilla, then we drove through the mountains. It sure was a long, lonely ride for me between The Dalles and Pendleton. Nothing but prairie and the sage brush being blown around by the east winds.

In the loneliness, Mildred's mind began to wander back to the events of March 17. She knew when her mother began to reprimand her father about the milk separator he would respond in anger. He was often angry, but then again, her mother was often scolding him. She wondered why two people who seemed to infuriate each other so much had married.

Mildred stared at the back of Uncle August and Aunt Elisabeth's heads. She had just met them when they came to help after her mother and Mabel had died, but they reminded her of the Millers who lived on the adjoining farm. Ida Miller was her father's cousin, and Mildred fondly remembered the Sunday dinners they'd shared at the Millers' home after attending services at the Lutheran church. Ida and Herman Miller were German immigrants like her parents, but that's where the similarities ended. The Millers were about ten years older than her parents, but had been married about twenty years longer, and all of the Miller children were older than Mildred and her sisters. The Millers' house was quite beautiful and well kept compared with the Flatau farm, a comparison that had become an irritant to her father.

The sound of crunching gravel startled Mildred from her thoughts as the car pulled to the side of the road.

"We're in the Blue Mountains, Mildred," said Uncle August as he opened the car door. Mildred noticed the sign ahead that read, "Blue Mountains – 3000 foot elevation." Uncle August got out of the car and walked around to the passenger side and opened the door for his wife, something Mildred had never seen her father do for her mother.

"Why don't we all take a little break and stretch our legs," said Aunt Elisabeth as she got out of the car. "We might as well open the picnic basket, too."

Mildred got out of the car, grabbed a sandwich and wandered over to the short wooden guardrail. Munching on her sandwich, she realized just how little she knew about her mother's sister and her husband.

She knew she had been given the middle name Elisabeth in honor of Aunt Elisabeth, and that Aunt Elisabeth was fifteen years younger than her mother. Aunt Elisabeth and her mother resembled one another, but Aunt Elisabeth was a little taller and much thinner, which Mildred assumed was because Aunt Elisabeth's body hadn't produced any children. Aunt Elisabeth sounded a lot like her mother, but softer in tone, although Mildred sensed that between her aunt and uncle, Aunt Elisabeth was in charge. As for Uncle August, he was a much shorter man than her father, but he stood much taller in Mildred's eyes due to his kind, gentle nature.

Aunt Elisabeth stepped beside Mildred and put her hand on Mildred's shoulder. "I'm going to give your Uncle August a break and drive for a while. Would you like to sit up front with me?"

"Oh, no thank you," replied Mildred and immediately wondered if she'd said the right thing.

Back on the road, Mildred continued sizing up her aunt and uncle. They'd been married just a little more than a year, and Mildred thought it must be quite an adjustment for them to have a teenager move into their home. It would be an adjustment for Mildred, as well, but she felt there was nothing she couldn't handle. After all, she'd handled her father, hadn't she?

Friday, March 17, 1933

Sandy Ridge – 7:50 a.m.

This argument between their parents had followed the same pattern of all the others Mildred and Mabel had witnessed. They were always heated and intense. But for some reason this time was different for their mother, and she finally declared, "I've had enough, Edward! I'm going to live with Frances."

Mildred and Mabel stopped eating, and stared at each other, unsure what do to.

Anna stomped up the stairs and motioned for Mildred and Mabel to follow. They dutifully obeyed, relieved that the yelling was over, at least for now.

As they marched up the stairs they were unaware that Edward had reached his limit, as well.

"Mildred, get the suitcase," ordered her mother, who was beginning to gather clothes from the dresser drawers. Mildred did as she was told and laid the suitcase on the bed. But then what? Were she and Mabel supposed to go to school? Were they supposed to help their mother pack? What did this mean for them? Uncertain, they sat on the bed and waited for further instructions.

Anna's packing was briefly interrupted by Edward.

"Anna?"

"Leave, Edward!"

As they continued to watch her mother pack, Mildred wondered whether her father was trying to apologize, or whether he just wanted to continue arguing.

Edward interrupted again, "Anna?"

"Edward, leave us alone!"

"Fine! Go ahead – leave! I wish you'd left twenty years ago!" Edward shouted as he stomped down the stairs.

"Twenty-three," muttered Anna under her breath.

Mildred felt a hand on her leg and jumped a little.

"I'm sorry to wake you, but we're in Ontario, Mildred," whispered Aunt Elisabeth.

Uncle August was already out of the car and heading into the hotel to register.

Mildred looked up at her aunt in surprise. She hadn't intended to fall asleep. Her letter to Frances was still in her lap. Was I dreaming about the argument, Mildred wondered to herself.

"Oh, that's alright," Mildred responded sleepily. "I'll get my things."

When Uncle August returned to the car, he began unloading their suitcases. As he handed her suitcase to her she was reminded that it was the same suitcase she'd retrieved for her mother. The suitcase her mother had packed to leave her father. Aunt Elisabeth put her hand on Mildred's shoulder once again as they walked toward the entrance of the hotel. It was the second time that day Mildred had experienced her aunt's warm gesture, but Mildred still felt cold.

Mildred had never stayed in a hotel before, and before March 17, she would have loved the escape from the norm. Now, though, all she longed for was the predictable routine of her former life. Yes, that life had been scary at times, but it was familiar, which was oddly comforting.

Mildred and Aunt Elisabeth walked to their room and changed into their nightgowns as Uncle August made sure the car was secure for the night.

"Let's say our prayers, Mildred," said Aunt Elisabeth.

"Now the light has gone away. Father, listen while I pray. Asking You to watch and keep and to grant me quiet sleep," whispered Mildred. She paused thinking about the last two words. Nights had been long and sleep had been elusive in the past few weeks. When she had slept, nightmares had made peaceful slumber impossible. Just as in the car, she had slept but her mind had been actively remembering the awful events of March 17.

Aunt Elisabeth continued the prayer. "Jesus Savior, wash away all that has been wrong today." Mildred joined her. "Make me more like You each day in all that I do and say. Amen."

Mildred caught a glimpse of the clock as she crawled between the sheets. It was 1 a.m. A long day of riding in the car had been exhausting, and before long, she could feel herself drift off.

◆ Lodging in Ontario, Oregon ◆

According to Mildred's diary, she, Uncle August and Aunt Elisabeth spent the first night of their road trip in Ontario, Oregon. Mildred didn't indicate the name of the hotel, but the Malheur County Historical Society was gracious enough to provide not only information regarding the lodging available to the trio in 1933, but also this picture of the Hotel Ontario, which was built in 1905. It was located on Oregon Street.

They also provided information on the Moore Hotel, which was built 1910-1911. According to the historical society, it was very famous in its day, also housing a restaurant and barbershop. The following article was written about the local landmark when it burned. I've included it with the permission of Stephanie Spiess, publisher of the *Argus Observer*.

Losing a landmark

1995 inferno wipes out remaining vestiges of once grand hotel

BY JESSICA KELLER
ARGUS OBSERVER

Aug 3, 2008

City emergency service personnel stand at a distance as the blazing inferno that wiped out the Moore Hotel for good in 1995 smoldered. While the hotel had long been abandoned, the building had once been an elegant and popular establishment that provided travelers to Ontario with a place to stay and the community a place to gather.

ONTARIO — Night had settled in Ontario when flames erupted in a vacant downtown building on Oregon Street sometime before 11 p.m. Friday, Oct. 13, 1995. Within a couple of hours the fire turned into an inferno that swallowed the whole of the building, and by Saturday, a longtime Ontario landmark — the once imposing and grand Moore Hotel — was reduced to rubble.

While the building had been vacant since 1984, after another fire severely damaged the interior, the blaze in 1995 wiped away the remainder of the building that had persevered and evolved since Ontario's early days, making it one of the top historical events of Ontario's 125 years of history.

The Glory Days

The Moore Hotel was built in 1910 and 1911 by prominent Ontario businessman T.H. Moore just as Ontario was beginning to take its shape as a regional hub for Eastern Oregon and western Idaho. While originally more modest in size than it later became, with 45 rooms to start that soon grew to 60, the hotel was designed as a more upscale establishment that catered to the numbers of people who came to Ontario daily at the time to take their ranch livestock to auction or conduct other business.

As a girl, former editor of the Argus Observer Chris Moore, who went on to marry T.H. Moore's grandson Bill, stayed at the hotel a number of times when her family traveled from their ranch in Jordan Valley so her father could do business in the area. She laughs when she remembers dining in the establishment's grand dining room with her mother, two younger brothers and sister.

She said the restaurant was fancy, with nice tablecloths, plates and silverware and even finger bowls. Moore said she and her siblings did not know what the little bowls sitting on the tables were, so their mother explained they were supposed to dip their fingers in the bowls and dry them off with a napkin before eating.

"Well, my brothers weren't about to do that, and I just pretended to," she said.

Moore also said the hotel had a "fantastic, huge" fire place in the "enormous" main lobby that was faced with Indian artifacts and fossils.

A large room used for dances and large meetings and conventions was situated next to the dining room, and throughout, she said, nice wooden furniture and other pieces, some antiques at the time and all antique now, decorated the building.

"It was kind of the showplace of southeast Oregon," she said. "And it was a fashionable thing to stay at the Moore Hotel, and it was quite plush."

While popular for cattlemen's conventions and other ranchers and farmers to stay at, the hotel became a gathering place for the local community as well, Moore said. The hotel also housed the local bus depot in the 1940s through 1960s.

The later years

Through the years the hotel had been remodeled a number of times. The last major renovation took place in 1975.

Former Ontario Fire Chief Randy Simpson, now deputy state fire marshal, said he remembers going to the lounge in the bottom floor of the building as a 21-year-old and the place being packed with people. He also said other businesses were situated in the building, which the Moore family had sold, as well, and it was always busy.

The hotel was hit by two fires in the early 1980s, and Simpson was at both, responding as a firefighter. The first was put out quickly and caused minor damage, he said. The second caused extensive damage, Simpson said, and led to its closure.

The building then sat vacant for a number of years, and the abandoned building became an eyesore, with plywood across the entrances to keep out homeless people looking for shelter and others causing mischief.

That infrequently worked, however, as Ontario Police Chief Mike Keep, who was then a patrolman, recalls.

"We would go in there sometimes at night and chase folks out," he said. "So it wasn't uncommon for people to be in there."

The building had gotten to be such a problem, city officials and downtown businessmen discussed the state of the structure and what should be done to remedy the situation. According to an October 1995 Argus Observer article, the city manager at the time, the police chief and downtown business community members agreed at a meeting Oct. 3, the building was an "eyesore" and recommended the building be torn down and a rehabilitation effort launched on that section of the street.

Coincidentally or ironically, perhaps both, the building burned down 10 days later, and by Oct. 14, a crane from Boise was already dismantling what was left of the building.

The fire

When the final fire struck, Moore was completely unaware — sleeping peacefully in her bed. She, instead, heard the news from a friend the next morning, and she and her husband, who has since died, broke the news to his mother, who was very fond of the building, Moore said.

"My husband and I were really shocked and unhappy," she said.

Kee and Simpson remember the fire very well, however. According to the Oct. 1, 1995, Argus Observer, the fire was reported by a police officer on patrol who saw white smoke billowing from the buildings. The fire department arrived shortly after, and Simpson, who was then deputy fire chief, said all or almost all neighboring fire departments arrived on mutual aid soon after that.

Simpson was one of the first firemen to enter the building through the basement door next to the alley, and he said, by that time, the fire had already spread to other levels of the five-story structure.

"We had heavy, heavy smoke boiling out of all the floors," he said, adding the heaviest fire was in the basement and was probably the largest amount of fire contained in one building that he has seen during his career.

He said, when he and a few others entered they saw a 4-inch cast iron pipe glowing red and sagging, it was that hot.

When Simpson and his crew turned a nozzle to the ceiling, a big chunk of charred ceiling fell down on the floor, and the firefighters knew it was time to beat a hasty retreat because nothing could be done for the building. Instead they directed their attention to preventing the fire from spreading to neighboring buildings.

Once on fire, he said, the structure was ripe for disaster because an elevator shaft that ran through the center of the building acted as a flue, carrying the fire up from the basement quickly.

"It was just a nice little chimney for it," he said.

Simpson said the north wall of the building collapsed early in the morning, and it was fortunate no firefighters were under that section at the time, although bricks did hit a few of Simpson's crew, who were standing across the street.

Meanwhile, city police officers were at the perimeters of the scene keeping people and vehicles away through the night. A large crowd of more than 100 people flocked to the scene and watched the spectacle, Kee said.

It was a sad ending, Kee and Simpson both said, but both pointed out the building had been vacant for a long time before then and was no longer the crowning glory of Ontario's landmarks.

"And, unfortunately, for it to be abandoned that many years, it lost the aura that it had," Simpson said.

He said, while they could never prove it and eventually labeled the circumstances behind the fire as unknown, fire officials suspected people had something to do with the start of the blaze, either setting it by accident or intentionally.

Moore, whose family has only memories, some pieces of furniture and photos, said Ontario lost more than just a building when the Moore Hotel burned down.

"It lost a fair-sized part of history," she said. "It was a landmark."

Chapter Two
Idaho - Wednesday, April 12, 1933

Mildred awakened to stirring in the dark hotel room. She opened her eyes and could see Uncle August and Aunt Elisabeth had already dressed. Aunt Elisabeth was making the bed and Uncle August was snapping shut their suitcase. Mildred felt like she had just fallen asleep. It couldn't be morning already.

"What time is it?" Mildred asked trying not to sound groggy.

"It's a little past five," answered Uncle August. "Aunt Elisabeth is anxious to get back on the road. She's a stickler for keeping to a schedule."

"Oh, go put things in the car so Mildred can get dressed," instructed Aunt Elisabeth. "Then meet us in the diner for breakfast.

When Uncle August left the room, Mildred slipped out of bed and quickly dressed. She wished she could have slept longer. For the first time in a long time she hadn't dreamed. Maybe it was because she was too tired to dream. Maybe, she wondered, it was because she was putting more miles between herself and the incident. Maybe once she arrived in Detroit she could simply sleep and have real rest.

Mildred noticed the thermometer as they sat down at the hotel diner. The sight of 28 degrees made her shiver, but the hot oatmeal warmed her from the inside out. Oatmeal with warm milk reminded her of the many breakfasts she'd shared with her sisters as they got ready for school. She smiled at the memory of how annoyed Frances became with little Mabel, who ate so slowly.

Mildred glanced out the diner window. The sun was starting to rise and it looked like the skies were going to be sunny and clear. She wasn't looking forward to another long day in the car, but she finished her oatmeal quickly. She didn't want her aunt and uncle to be waiting for her.

"Today we drive through Idaho," said Uncle August trying to sound cheerful and excited as they left the diner.

All too soon they were back on the road putting more distance between her and home. She tried to occupy herself by continuing her letter to Frances.

We left Ontario this morning at 6:15 a.m. We're almost to the Snake River. That's the river that creates a border between Oregon and Idaho. I wish you were with us, Frances.

Mildred couldn't focus on the letter as loneliness for everything familiar flooded over her. She needed to hold back the tears. "No crying," she told herself. The stomachache she'd been experiencing for weeks had returned. Should she tell Aunt Elisabeth? No, she didn't want to be a bother to her and Uncle August. They were so kind to come so far to be with her and Frances when they needed them so badly and to take her in.

She wondered what living in Detroit with her aunt and uncle would be like. She really knew very little about them. Although they were newlyweds, Uncle August and Aunt Elisabeth weren't a young couple. Aunt Elisabeth was thirty-eight years old and Uncle August was fifty-one. They were both German immigrants like her parents and the Millers. Aunt Elisabeth arrived in the United States in 1914 when she was about twenty years old. She worked as a private nurse. Uncle August came to the United States as a boy in 1888. He had been married before, but his wife of nearly twenty years had died about a year before he married Aunt Elisabeth. Mildred wondered if maybe Aunt Elisabeth had been a nurse for Uncle August's late wife.

Mildred wanted to ask about Detroit, but she was still a little shy about initiating conversation with her aunt.

Mildred knew Detroit was a big city – bigger than Portland. Mildred had only known farm life in the small town of Sandy. She wondered how she would fit in at her new school and neighborhood. Her school in Sandy was filled with other students who also lived on farms. Only a few of her classmates lived in town. She'd never lived in a neighborhood where the houses were close together. The Millers were their closest neighbors, but there were acres of fields between their houses.

Even today, the houses in Mildred's Sandy neighborhood are separated by fields. This picture is taken from the approximate former location of the Flatau's barn. The Millers' home was located in the upper right-hand side of the photo in front of the tree line.

Thinking of the Millers brought the awful memories to the surface and Mildred's stomachache became more severe. She continued her letter to Frances, hoping to free her mind of the tragic events.

We just went through Glenns Ferry, Idaho, and are driving through the mountains.

A loud bang and mild jerk shook Mildred from her letter writing. It didn't take long to realize they'd crashed into another vehicle. Uncle August got out of the car to inspect the damage and talk to the driver of the other car. While Mildred didn't want anything bad to happen, she was grateful for the distraction and a little excitement.

"Well, this will put us behind schedule, at the very least," said Aunt Elisabeth.

Mildred assumed she was talking to her, but not knowing how to respond just murmured, "Uh-huh."

A few moments later Uncle August returned to the car. "They just have some minor damage – nothing to worry about. They're traveling from New Mexico. I think we should head back to Glenns Ferry and have a mechanic take a look at our car, though. There's a lot of distance between here and home and we want to make sure the car is safe."

"I guess it can't be helped," said Aunt Elisabeth. "We'll just arrive in Pocatello later than we'd planned."

Aunt Elisabeth's words made Mildred realize the long day in the car had just become longer if they were going to stick to Aunt

Elisabeth's schedule. However, she might get a chance to explore some of Glenns Ferry and that sounded fun.

The trio returned to Glenns Ferry and found the local garage. It was about noon and the temperature was much warmer, so as the car was being checked out Mildred and Aunt Elisabeth walked along the street in front of the garage.

"Oh, here's a little market," said Aunt Elisabeth. "If I can find something we can eat on the road, maybe we can get back on schedule."

"Can I just walk along the street?" Mildred asked. "I won't go far."

"Okay, but stay close by," admonished Aunt Elisabeth. "We want to get back on the road as soon as the car is ready."

Aunt Elisabeth walked into the market, and Mildred continued down the sidewalk, enjoying the warmth of the sun. Glenns Ferry was larger than Sandy, but not as big as Portland. Mildred noticed the train tracks and railway depot and thought the trains must travel to Detroit. Maybe she could have taken the train to Detroit all by herself. Uncle August and Aunt Elisabeth wouldn't have even had to come to Oregon. Mildred thought about what it must be like traveling by train. A trip from Portland to Detroit would take a long time, although it must be faster than by car. She wondered if riding a train was just like she'd read about in books with special cars for eating and sleeping.

"Mildred," shouted Uncle August.

Mildred ran back to the garage and her Uncle August. "Is the car ready?"

"The mechanic just finished – nothing major," Uncle August glanced around. "Where's Elisabeth?"

"She went into the market to get some food for lunch," Mildred answered.

Just then, Aunt Elisabeth walked out of the market. "Is the car finished?" she asked.

"They think it will be fine," said Uncle August. "Did you get us something to eat?"

"Some sliced meat and cheese should hold us until we get to Pocatello and stop for the night," reasoned Aunt Elisabeth. "Let's get back on the road. We've lost at least an hour."

They hurried back into the car and were on the road again. Mildred wished the trip wasn't so rushed, but understood Aunt Elisabeth's schedule would help Uncle August get back to work. He had already taken off a lot of time to travel to Oregon.

She wished she could have taken the train. It was probably too expensive, but what an adventure. Mildred imagined herself riding in the train, observing other passengers and listening to the sounds of the wheels against the tracks and the whistle as they arrived at each stop. Some passengers would get off and others would get on. With so much to see and hear, she doubted there would be any time to think about her mother and Mabel.

Mildred was only slightly aware of Uncle August muttering about the steering wheel. "It seems loose," he complained. "We'd better stop in Buhl and have it tightened. "

Mildred was glad to have something interesting to write in her letter to Frances. She began describing the car accident.

A dish and one of our suitcases broke when we crashed. We had the car fixed at Glenns Ferry and traveled on to Buhl. We stopped to get the steering wheel tightened, which gave me a chance to have a swell talk with a man from Philadelphia. You meet such interesting people on the road. It's 83 miles to Pocatello. I think that's where we're spending the night. Uncle August thinks we'll be there around 8 p.m.

Uncle August stopped the car. "We're in Thousand Springs," he announced.

Mildred was surprised they were making a stop since they were behind schedule due to the accident.

Uncle August asked, "Do you want to see an artesian well?"

Mildred nodded her head, although she was curious about what made a well worth stopping to see. Her father had dug their well on the farm by hand, making sure it was as perfectly round as possible and deep. She'd pumped water from it many times.

The capped well. According to neighbors it was hand dug by Edward Flatau.

Mildred saw right away what was special about artesian wells – the water just bubbled to the surface on its own! It looked so clean and pure, unlike the water from their well that had been declared unsanitary by a state inspector just before…

Aunt Elisabeth interrupted Mildred's thoughts. "What do you think of the artesian well, Mildred?"

"I like a well you don't have to pump," replied Mildred. "I'll have to take some pictures for Frances." She took some pictures of the well and then some of the surrounding prairie.

While Mildred took pictures, Uncle August spoke quietly to his wife. "Thank you for understanding that Mildred is more important than our schedule."

Elisabeth smiled slightly. "Okay, Mildred. It's time to get back on the road," she said as she herded them back to the car, determined to get to Pocatello to spend the night.

Mildred was feeling more comfortable with her aunt and uncle, but still wished Frances was with them. She preferred looking out the window over trying to make conversation, but there really wasn't much to see driving through the Idaho prairie. No sooner had that thought crossed her mind, when she wished she could rid her mind of the view on the side of the road.

"Look at all those poor dead rabbits," exclaimed Aunt Elisabeth

"They must have been hit by cars," assumed Uncle August.

So many dead rabbits. So much death thought Mildred.

Friday, March 17, 1933

Sandy Ridge – 8:10 a.m.

Mildred and Mabel continued to watch their mother pack, still uncertain about what they were supposed to do. They both grasped that their lives were about to change, but to what extent, neither of them could imagine.

Anna finished filling the suitcase and snapped it shut. "It's time to leave, girls," she said. Even at that point, Mildred didn't know if she was to leave for Portland with her mother or merely leave the house and head to school.

Anna was resolute as she made her way downstairs. Mildred and Mabel followed.

"The girls are going to school and I'm leaving," Anna announced.

As Anna led the girls to the front door, Edward stepped in front of them blocking their way.

"Fine, Edward," her mother shouted. "We'll use the back door!"

Mildred, Mabel, and their mother turned to walk through the small house to the back door as her father ran out the front door, concealing the revolver he had grabbed from a drawer downstairs. As they stepped onto the back porch, Edward appeared from around the corner. Without a word he lifted the revolver and shot his wife in the mouth. Anna stumbled backwards from the impact, blood gushing from the facial wound.

Mildred and Mabel were stunned, but neither had time to process what had happened before their father turned the revolver on Mabel, shooting her through the head at point blank range. Mabel's lifeless body crumpled to the ground at the base of the back porch stairs.

Aunt Elisabeth's voice startled Mildred. "It looks like it's starting to snow."

Mildred, determined to shut the memories out of her mind for the evening, returned to writing her letter to Frances.

> *We hit snow in Twin Falls and it got worse as we drove through American Falls. We should arrive in Pocatello soon. We'll be spending the night at the St. Marie Hotel. Doesn't that sound grand!*

Mildred wondered if Frances would be able to tell from the letter that she was trying to sound like she was on vacation rather than moving to a far off place she really didn't want to call home. She was grateful that Uncle August and Aunt Elisabeth had offered to let her live with them, but she just wished it hadn't been necessary. She should be home in Sandy finishing the school year with her friends, laughing with Mabel and working on the farm. Why did her father have to destroy everything? Why was he so unreasonable and angry? Why was he, dare she think it, evil?

Mildred's stomachache returned. She knew she had to stop asking the unanswerable questions. It had been a long, eventful day. They would be arriving in Pocatello soon and would check into the St. Marie Hotel for the night where she hoped sleep would be an escape from her thoughts.

She leaned forward, and by the light of the headlamps watched the snow fall.

◆ The St. Marie Hotel ◆

"I was born in a trunk in the Princess Theater in Pocatello, Idaho..."

While the Princess Theater is the fictional birthplace of Judy Garland's character in the movie, "A Star is Born," it is a real place. The theater was housed in the St. Marie Hotel where Mildred, Uncle August, and Aunt Elisabeth spent their second night on their road trip from Oregon to Michigan.

According to the Pocatello, Idaho, Historical Society, the hotel was originally built as the St. Marie, but became the Hotel Nicolett in the early 1900s. The name "St. Marie" is etched in stone on the building in a picture from 1913. The name changed, but perhaps Mildred referred to it as the St. Marie because the name was on the building.

The hotel was renamed the Whitman and remodeled in the 1930s by local architect Frank Paradice.

The Princess Theater was housed in it when it was known as the Hotel Nicolett.

The hotel as it looks today. "St. Marie" had been etched where "The Whitman" is now visible.

Photo courtesy of Darcy Hale, resident of Pocatello, Idaho.

Chapter Three
Wyoming - Thursday, April 13, 1933

Mildred had slept fitfully, and was exhausted. She mindlessly dressed and went downstairs for breakfast, making a mental note to mention the magnificent staircase in her letter to Frances. Normally she would have enjoyed the luxury of staying in a hotel like the St. Marie, but her life was far from normal. She wondered if it would ever be normal again.

The three ate breakfast quickly and in silence. Mildred assumed her aunt and uncle were as tired as she was. Aunt Elisabeth wanted to be on the road by 6 a.m., and Mildred sensed the need to move more quickly as she helped load the car.

They headed out of Pocatello fifteen minutes behind schedule with a lot of snow and ice on the pavement. Mildred's eyes were glued to the road, partly because of the treacherous driving conditions and partly because she didn't want her mind to wander back to the events of March 17. The last thing Mildred wanted was for her stomachache to return. As long as she focused on other things, keeping her mind occupied, she felt fine. The moment she began to recall the horror of that day, she noticed the stomachache.

For the next 100 miles, Mildred occupied her thoughts with the weather conditions. She tried focusing on the sound of the snow crunching under the weight of the car. It sort of reminded her of cows chewing grass, but not exactly. She thought about how snow makes everything look perfect. It comes down and lays a clean, white blanket over the ground, covering any imperfections. Every field looks the same. It doesn't matter if your harvest is good or bad or whether you've cultivated and planted correctly. It doesn't matter if you are rich or poor, and it doesn't matter if your family is normal or crazy; everything looks perfect when covered with snow.

Mildred felt a little chill and pulled her grey wool coat tighter around her and continued to watch the road. The snow was tapering off, and Uncle August seemed less tense as he continued to drive.

"Welcome to Wyoming, Mildred," said Aunt Elisabeth. "We're one state closer to home."

Mildred managed a smile, but was still exhausted from the lack of sleep. She could take a nap, but didn't want to take the chance that she might have a nightmare. Perhaps she could continue her letter to Frances, but before she could get out paper and pencil, Aunt Elisabeth interrupted.

"Look at all those sheep!"

Mildred had never seen so many sheep and for the next five miles, Mildred, Uncle August, and Aunt Elisabeth counted sheep. They'd get to 100 and start over. Someone must live nearby to care for the animals, but they didn't see a house, or even a barn.

"Whoa," exclaimed Uncle August as the pavement ended and the road became nothing but hardened dirt covered by snow and ice. He gripped the steering wheel more tightly, but the road was so slippery they began to slide. Mildred was afraid they might have another accident, but Uncle August brought the car under control.

For the next fifty miles they sat quietly, as if silently willing the car to stay on the slick country road.

Just as suddenly as the pavement ended, it returned, startling them all.

The rest of the drive through Wyoming was uneventful. They passed an occasional car, but the area was pretty desolate – not a single house for miles.

Mildred thought things must not have been much different when cowboys traveled through Wyoming. This trip by car had been tough at times, but what if they were traveling by horse and wagon, or having to sleep under the stars? The Wild West always sounded like fun, but experiencing how uninhabited and lonely and cold this area could be, Mildred was glad she lived in the 20th century. Maybe the loneliness is what made cowboys sing.

Cowboys singing made her think of Mabel. Funny girl, always singing cowboy songs.

O bury me not on the lone prairie
Where the wild coyotes may howl over me
Where the buffalo roams and the winds blow free
O bury me not on the lone prairie

I want to be laid where mothers' prayers
And sisters' tears will mingle there
Where friends will come and weep over me
O bury me not on the lone prairie

Mildred couldn't get the sound of Mabel singing that song out of her head. Over and over it played in her mind. "I should have been able to do something," thought Mildred. "I should have..." Mildred's thoughts stopped. She'd already had this conversation with herself and it led nowhere. There was nothing that could have been done. She was alive and her mother and Mabel were dead. For some unexplainable reason, she had survived.

Friday, March 17, 1933

Sandy Ridge – 8:12 a.m.

Mildred was petrified. It was surreal – a bad nightmare. Seeing her bleeding mother crawl toward Mabel's body brought her to reality. Her father had gone mad, and would kill them all.

As Edward came at her with the gun, she instinctively grabbed his arm and screamed out the first thing that came to her mind. "Christ is watching you," she exclaimed. "You can't do this!"

"I can't help myself," Edward replied. "I am a murderer."

"I pray you don't shoot me," Mildred pleaded.

Edward lowered the gun. Mildred's heart was racing and she was short of breath.

Thinking the violence had ended, Anna, bleeding and weak, picked up the limp body of her youngest daughter Mabel. Carrying her on her back, she headed for the road determined to get help.

Mildred couldn't move or speak. She was completely frozen.

Her father stood silent for a moment, but then turned and relentlessly chased after his wounded wife.

Mildred was left alone on the back porch. She was trying to understand all that had just happened when she heard two shots ring out. She shuddered at the sound.

Edward had shot Anna twice in the stomach. Feeling like he had finished what he started, he returned to the back porch.

When Mildred saw her father, she assumed he'd killed her mother. He appeared less agitated, but she was still terrified when he told her to go inside the house and sit down. She obeyed and Edward followed her inside.

He looked at Mildred and took in a deep breath, then let it out slowly. "I'm going to spare your life. Don't watch where I go," he commanded.

Without another word, Edward walked out the back door.

As soon as she heard her father step off the back porch, Mildred got up and ran through the front door toward the road where her mother had collapsed. She was relieved and grateful to see their neighbor and former farmhand Paul Buuck.

"Oh, Paul," Mildred managed to squeak out. She saw her mother slightly move and heard her groaning in pain. Her mother was still alive!

Paul looked at her, not knowing what to say, yet knowing he had to get help.

She knew help had come too late for Mabel, but she prayed her mother's life could be saved. She looked at her mother's pale face and blue gingham dress stained with blood. Mildred bent over her mother and managed a slight smile of reassurance, but she seriously doubted her mother would recover.

Paul had summoned another neighbor, Leif Anderson, who brought his car to the Flatau driveway.

"Where's Edward?" asked Mr. Anderson as he got out of his car.

"In the back field, I think," said Paul.

Both men worked quickly and gently to load Anna and Mabel in the backseat of the car. Mildred noticed Art Skogan walking up the road on this way to school. He was in Mabel's grade.

"Art," Paul called out. "You need to turn around and go back home. Hurry!"

The young boy seemed confused, but obeyed, turning around and running back to his home.

"Come on, Mildred," said Paul. "You can ride up front with us."

Mildred got in the front seat between Paul and Mr. Anderson. As they headed to Sandy for help a few miles away, Mildred caught sight of her father stumbling west over the grassy field toward the Millers' home.

She didn't know if she should say something to Paul and Mr. Anderson. If her father was going to harm the Millers, someone should warn them. She glanced back at her mother. Warning the Millers would have to wait. Her mother needed medical help before it was too late.

Mildred desperately wanted to think of something else and worked up the nerve to finally ask Aunt Elisabeth about Detroit.

"It's a very beautiful city with tree-lined streets and parks," said Aunt Elisabeth. "Uncle August has lived there since shortly after arriving in this country. I just moved there from Chicago a little more than a year ago when we got married. We live in the German neighborhood.

"Only German people live in your neighborhood?"

"Well, I suppose people from other countries live there, but it's mostly Germans," explained Aunt Elisabeth. "There's a Polish neighborhood and an Irish neighborhood, too."

"Is your church in your neighborhood," Mildred asked.

"It's just a short street car ride. The services are in German, just like your Lutheran church in Sandy, but it's a Baptist church," explained Aunt Elisabeth. "It's different, but you'll adjust."

Mildred didn't care if the church was Lutheran or not, or whether services were held in German or English. She was going to be attending church again regularly, and that made her happy.

"Is the school nearby? Can I walk there?"

"The bus that will take you to school runs one street over from our street, so you can wait for it at the intersection."

Mildred suddenly became very unsettled and asked, "Is it a big school?"

"It's larger than where you went to school in Sandy, but I'm sure you'll make friends quickly," assured Aunt Elisabeth. "Since I've only lived there a short time I have more to learn about the city. We'll discover Detroit together, Mildred."

Mildred felt excited and fearful at the same time. She enjoyed the thought of exploring a big city, but was afraid of all the change. She'd never been on a school bus before. She and her sisters had walked a little more than a mile south to their grade school. She and Frances had walked to their high school with other friends from the surrounding farms. They met as a group on the plank road that ran in front of their farm.

The thought of the plank road brought her back to her earlier thoughts of Paul helping Mr. Anderson load her mother and Mabel into the car. She wondered whether she would be able to think of that road without that memory rising to the surface and forcing out anything else.

"Ah, we made it to Rock River. This is where we'll spend the night," announced Uncle August.

The cold, harsh temperatures of Rock River matched her painfully intense memories. Mildred thought back to the image of her father trudging toward the Millers' farm. That was the last time she saw him.

It was difficult for Mildred to deal with the anger she felt for her father. He had taken so much from her and Frances, but Mildred knew that anger was what motivated her father, and she didn't want to be anything like him. She had relied on her faith on that day. And her faith helped her get through everything that happened afterward.

As she crawled into bed she silently prayed, "God, please help me to feel more love than hate."

◆ MILDRED'S FAITH ◆

Church was an important part of Mildred's life, but her personal faith that grew out of her church attendance became an integral part of who she was. As a person of faith, I can relate to Mildred's desire not only to be part of a church community, but also to live out the faith on a daily basis.

Some of my earliest memories are of the church my family attended for many years. When I refer to my family, I'm including my mother's parents, her sister and brother, and their families. My grandfather was a deacon for many years. My uncle was a deacon and youth leader. My mother was a Sunday school teacher and church pianist. My dad led the church choir for several years.

The church was not just a place of worship: it also served as part of our social community. My immediate family certainly had involvement in the community outside of church. My father was a volunteer firefighter for many years and my mother served on the Women's Auxiliary. She was also involved in our school, serving as a room mother and as part of the P.T.A. However, the one place where my entire extended family functioned together socially was the church.

In addition to my mother's side of the family, my dad was raised in a home that valued faith. My dad's mother died when he was quite young, so as was common in the 1930s, he was raised by his older sister and her husband, a pastor. Interaction with either side of the family usually involved some element of our faith.

It is with that point of view that I read Mildred's story. It is from that point of view that I wanted to understand her faith.

Immanuel Lutheran Church: Mildred's foundation of faith

Edward and Anna were married at Immanuel Lutheran Church in Sandy, May 22, 1910. Frances, Mildred, and Mabel were all baptized at Immanuel Lutheran Church. However, after Mabel's baptism in 1921, there is no record of the Flataus in the church history. Confirmation in the Lutheran faith usually takes place around age fourteen. Neither Frances nor Mildred is listed in the confirmation records, which appear to be well-kept. According to the records, their pastor, Rev. Dobberfuhl, officiated at 146 baptisms, 122 confirmations 27 weddings and 38 funerals during his twenty-three years of ministry in Sandy.

Interviewing Grace Reich, the granddaughter of Ida Miller, Edward Flatau's cousin, I learned of the Flatau family having Sunday dinner at the Miller home after church. The dinners ceased when Edward ended the family's church attendance.

Immanuel Lutheran Church and congregants in 1902. Some of the services were held in German, drawing many German immigrants who had moved to Sandy to work in the logging industry.

*The church moved to a larger facility built on Pleasant Street in
1959, but the original building still stands along Pioneer Street.*
Photos courtesy of Immanuel Lutheran Church.

*Reverend Frank Dobberfuhl served as pastor of Immanuel Lutheran
from 1904 to 1928.*
This was the time period the Flatau family attended the church.
Photo courtesy of Immanuel Lutheran Church

That Rev. Dobberfuhl left the community in 1928 and the Flataus had at some point stopped attending the church services could explain why Frances did not include the church in the funeral and burial services for her mother and sister. While she may have had a connection to Rev. Dobberfuhl, the Flataus were likely unfamiliar with his successor.

Ebenezer Baptist Church: Mildred's fostering of faith

Interestingly, Mildred's faith grew, in spite of the lack of formal church education and attendance. She began attending Ebenezer German American Baptist Church with her Uncle August and Aunt Elisabeth when she arrived in Detroit, Michigan. It was the church where she met her future husband, Gerald Cape, and where they attended with their adopted daughters, Geraldine and Danell.

According to church history, Ebenezer German American Baptist Church was founded in 1898 by a group of sixty German immigrants. They were motivated by their desire to hold some of their services in English in order to reach their neighbors, but the church of which they had been a part refused the opportunity. So these immigrants rented a hall in the heart of Detroit along Gratiot Avenue, and they named themselves Ebenezer German American Baptist Church.

Within a few weeks, the new congregation raised enough money to build a white frame structure just a few blocks away on the corner of Moran and Leland. That building is still standing today, just behind the Faygo plant on Gratiot. In their first ten years, the church membership tripled.

By the time Mildred arrived in Detroit to live with her Uncle August and Aunt Elisabeth, the church was located on Mt. Elliott at the corner of Canfield. According to the Detroit Historical Society the church was located "a few blocks north and 14 blocks west of their house on Parker Ave. Nearby Mack Avenue had a street car, so the trip to Mt. Elliott would have been short.

At that point the East Side was predominately German; however, the area around Mt. Elliott was in transition. Germans were gravitating further from the city center, and the neighborhood would have had a higher percentage of Belgians, Italians, Eastern Europeans and, gradually, African Americans. This was also a neighborhood close to several auto factories, and the residents would have been severely impacted by the Great Depression." The church history echoes this account.

The church continued to grow throughout the 1940s, and they hired their first non-German pastor. They also launched their first ministry to "positively influence youth in the community, serving Anthony Wayne Elementary School, which was located on the far edge of the city, miles to the northeast, near forests and wetlands surrounding a small road aptly named 'Moross.'"

The congregation eventually built a new church at a location near the school in the 1950s, where they hosted outdoor concerts and a series of rallies featuring a then unknown preacher named Billy Graham. The church sent buses into the new subdivisions every weekend, bringing hundreds of children into the church.

Grace Community Church, Detroit, Michigan.
Photo courtesy or Grace Community Church.

In the 1960s the church gained national recognition and their services were featured on radio broadcasts. They "took some heat" from other local churches for partnering with the Detroit African American Mission and publishing Dr. Martin Luther King, Jr.'s now famous "Letter from Birmingham Jail" in their monthly newsletter.

In 1991, the church changed its name to Grace Community Church to reflect that they were no longer serving just "Baptists."

Mildred's lifetime of service to the church appears to have mirrored the mission of the church: looking outside of themselves to meet the needs of others.

Upon my first hearing Mildred's story, I wanted to understand the faith of a young teen, still a few weeks shy of her sixteenth birthday. I wanted to understand how she was able to draw upon that complete faith in God to protect her from her father's rage. Even after spending years researching her story and talking with her relatives, I still don't comprehend it. Perhaps that level of faith is triggered when we need it most. Perhaps I don't understand it completely because I've been spared the type of tragedy Mildred endured. Nonetheless, I am in awe of her faith and admire her greatly.

Chapter Four
Nebraska – Friday, April 14, 1933

Mildred needed to stop the memories from overcoming her as they had the day before and decided to continue her letter to Frances.

> *We drove 200 miles yesterday through Wyoming without seeing a single house. Today we left Wyoming and entered Nebraska, and there wasn't much difference, but after about 25 miles we began to see more houses and corn fields. Uncle August says Nebraska and Iowa grow a lot of corn. The further we drive, the more pleasant it seems. You'll see, Frances. It will be more pleasant for you, too.*

Mildred began to feel guilty about leaving Frances back in Oregon. The circumstances were overwhelming, especially for a nineteen-year-old girl, but Mildred knew Frances was strong. They'd both been strong in the aftermath of their father's rage. "The red saga of Sandy Ridge" and "Berserk farmer kills wife and child" was how *The Oregonian* newspaper described the events.

Not only did she and Frances have to deal with the death of their mother and sister, but the revelation of their violent home life. Their stoic German heritage taught them to keep their less than idyllic home life private. No one must know what went on behind closed doors. The world outside must think they were a normal, hardworking, productive German family.

Mildred smiled remembering the days before her parents' arguments became severe. They had attended the Lutheran church with other community members, including the Millers. Services were always conducted in German. After church they ate Sunday dinner at the Millers' home. Those were happier times, although Frances, Mildred, and Mabel were embarrassed when their mother would "remind" their father about certain chores that needed to be done in front of the Millers. Mildred always winced a little at her mother's words, knowing they would all pay for the ill-timed conversation later at home.

When Mildred's father sensed that people in the church gossiped about his marriage, family, and less than successful farming, he demanded they stop attending church. The Lutheran church had been a huge part of their social life. Edward and Anna were married there, and all three girls had been baptized in the church, as well. It was an important part of Mildred's life and she missed learning about God. Without that religious teaching, Mildred doubted she would have had the faith to stand up to her father on that fateful day.

Where did that faith come from, Mildred wondered? They hadn't attended church for many years, and they no longer had Sunday dinner with the Millers. But her belief in God ran deep, and somehow she just knew she had to confront her father with what she knew to be true: God was watching everything and He would protect her.

Friday, March 17, 1933

Sandy Ridge - 8:30 a.m.

Edward continued walking across the field toward the home of his cousin Ida Miller and her husband Herman. Their immaculate home and farm had been a thorn in his side long enough. The Millers and their twenty-two-year-old son Otto saw Edward heading their direction. They'd called the police after hearing the gun shots earlier.

"Ida, come! Hurry!" Herman admonished his wife as they and Otto made their way to the home of neighbors George and Bertha Gunderson a quarter-mile away across the creek.

Ida kept looking down toward her cousin's home wondering about Anna and the girls. She wanted to ask Herman what he thought had happened, but was afraid her husband might confirm her worst fears. She silently prayed as they hurried down the gully and across the creek to the Gunderson home.

George Gunderson heard the knock at the door and grabbed his shotgun. He and Bertha had heard the gunshots earlier and were taking no chances.

"George! Open the door!"

George opened the door when he recognized Herman Miller's voice.

Bertha looked at the trembling Ida. "What's going on?" she demanded.

"We don't know," Herman answered, "but we heard the gunshots coming from the Flataus and called the police. We saw Edward headed this direction, and I wanted to get Ida some place safe."

Edward had seen them flee through the trees as he arrived at the Millers' property, but let them go without a confrontation. "I'll deal with them later," he muttered to himself. He wandered through the outbuildings until he found some gasoline. Yes, that's what he needed. He entered the Millers' home and began to spill out a little gasoline in every room. After today, that house would no longer be a reminder of his cousin's success and his own failure.

Bertha Gunderson took Ida into the kitchen and left the men to discuss the situation.

"George, I'm afraid Edward has done something awful. I don't want Ida going back to our house until the police have taken care of this," confided Herman.

"She can stay with us," George assured Herman.

As Herman and Otto left the Gunderson home, Herman instructed his son to head into town for help. Herman feared for his property, but didn't want to confront Edward. He followed Otto to the road, and then worked his way back to his property, keeping a safe distance.

Constable's office - 8:40 a.m.

Mildred, Paul, and Mr. Anderson arrived at the one-room office of W.G. Duncan, Constable for the town of Sandy. Mr. Anderson remained in the car with Anna while Paul and Mildred rushed in and asked Constable Duncan to call the town doctor.

"My mother's outside in the car. She's been shot. Please hurry," begged Mildred.

Constable Duncan didn't hesitate or ask questions. He had received the phone calls from concerned neighbors, but as a one-person force, he knew he couldn't handle such a situation and had contacted state and county law enforcement.

While Constable Duncan called the doctor, Mildred walked to the office door as if to check on her mother. Paul paced the floor. He'd been working on the Flataus' farm until Edward abruptly discharged him the day before. If he'd been there, maybe he could have stopped Edward, he thought.

"The doctor will be here very soon," Constable Duncan assured Mildred as he hung up the phone. "I received a lot of phone calls from your neighbors. The state police and deputy sheriffs should be arriving at your farm soon. If you'd like to wait outside for the doctor, Paul can give me the details of what happened.

Mildred felt relieved that the police might be able to stop her father from harming anyone else.

Mildred walked back to the car to wait for the doctor. She crawled into the front seat and looked at her mother. "The doctor will be here soon, Mother," she whispered. Anna barely groaned an acknowledgment.

Within ten minutes, the doctor had arrived and did what he could to help stabilize Anna, but he was not hopeful.

Mildred followed the doctor back inside the constable's office, while Mr. Anderson stayed with her mother.

"Constable, I think they'd better drive to Oregon City and get Mrs. Flatau to the hospital as soon as possible," said the doctor. "I'll call ahead so the hospital knows what to expect."

"I understand," replied Constable Duncan. Turning to Mildred he took a deep breath and informed Mildred of what she would need to do. "I know this is hard, Mildred, and I'm really sorry, but the sooner you give a formal statement about what happened, the better."

Mildred wasn't sure what that meant. "I need to help Mother first," she stammered

"I understand. I'll have the deputy sheriffs meet you at the hospital," said Constable Duncan.

Paul and Mildred hurried out the door to Mr. Anderson's car and were surprised to see Otto Miller.

"Are you alright, Mildred," Otto asked.

"We're taking Mother to the hospital," replied Mildred, not really answering Otto's question.

Paul asked Otto to have Otto's parents meet Mildred at the hospital in Oregon City. Paul knew the Millers were the only family Mildred had, except for Frances. He couldn't imagine how Frances was going to react. Someone was going to have to call her and break the news.

"Mildred, I need to go back home and take care of something," said Paul. "I'll try to get to the hospital later."

Mildred mindlessly nodded. She just wanted Mr. Anderson to drive as fast as possible and get her mother the help she needed. Mr. Anderson wanted Mildred to focus on something other than her mother.

"It's going to be okay, Mildred," said Mr. Anderson. "Otto said he could hear sirens as he left the farm. I guess a lot of our neighbors heard the gun shots and telephoned the police."

She nodded again, remembering what Constable Duncan had said.

Mildred felt a great sense of fear overwhelm her, although she was not sure why exactly. Was she frightened for her mother? Yes, but her fear was even bigger than the possibility of losing her mother. Was she afraid for her father? No. Whatever happened to him made little difference to her after today. Everything was out of control, and maybe that's what scared her the most.

Mildred told herself to stop being so frightened and focus. She needed to keep her mind clear so that when she met with the deputy sheriffs at the hospital she could give her statement. She knew she must keep calm and tell the story exactly how it happened. Maybe that was the only thing she could do to help her mother.

Sandy Ridge - 8:40 a.m.

On the outskirts of the small town of Sandy, state police and deputy sheriffs began descending on the Flatau farm. Led by State Patrolman R.N. Phillips, Sergeant Powell Clayton, Patrolmen G.D. Watkins, and K.C. Snow, they split up and began searching for Edward in the house, barn, and outbuildings on the property.

Unbeknownst to law enforcement, Edward was inside the Millers' home. He struck a match to the gasoline and the house exploded in a thunderous roar of fire that could be seen and heard for a quarter-mile.

When law enforcement heard the sound, and saw the smoke and flames billowing from the windows of the once beautiful home, they thought that's where they'd find Edward. Instinctively they slowly and carefully began moving across the open field toward the Millers' property, understanding their suspect was not only a murderer; he was now an arsonist who was bent on destroying anything or anyone who crossed the path of devastation he desired.

Edward was determined not just to destroy the Miller's home, but he wanted to destroy them as well. He knew they'd headed west, so he made his way toward the Gunderson farm believing that's where they'd gone to hide from him. Without encountering Herman Miller or the police, Edward walked down the gully toward the creek. As he stepped onto the footbridge, he was met by George Gunderson carrying his shotgun.

"You'd better stay away from here," Gunderson warned as he hitched his 12-guage shotgun a little higher.

Edward stopped and stared at him for a moment. George was known to be a proficient hunter and he knew how to use a gun. Understanding George wasn't making idle threats and would hit his intended target, Edward turned around and headed back to his farm.

Police cars were parked haphazardly alongside the road when Paul returned to his home across the street from the Flatau farm. The scene was bizarre, but Paul was focused on finding a phone number for Frances. Although he was a few years older, they had been classmates in school and he'd found her to be good company when he worked for her father building the Flatau's barn. Someone had to tell her what happened, and he thought it might be best coming from him.

Thinking of Paul brought a faint smile to Mildred's face. Even though her father had fired him for no reason, he still cared about her mother and her sisters. He and his family were good neighbors. Some of their other neighbors had provided unflattering information in the newspaper account. She'd read it so many times she almost had it memorized. In fact, a copy of the article was in her suitcase. Why she'd brought it with her, she didn't know. She'd read a quote from Mr. Gunderson describing her father as being in "great mental stress as he walked rapidly along the edge of the field, then in the brush and then in full view, wringing his hands and plucking at his sleeves." Was he insane, Mildred wondered? Was that what made him do it or had doing it driven him insane? Did it matter?

No, it didn't matter. No insight into why her father had erupted into a murderous rage would change the fact that her mother and little sister were dead.

A conversation between Uncle August and Aunt Elisabeth brought Mildred out of her thoughts.

"I think we've traveled far enough today," said Aunt Elisabeth.

"Yes, I think so," said Uncle August. "Grand Island sounds like a nice place to spend the night."

◆ W.G. DUNCAN ◆

Constable W.G. Duncan.
Permission to reprint granted by Sandy Historical Society.

The City of Sandy has grown quite a bit since the Flatau family resided here in 1933. What was a little town of about 300 in 1930, has grown to more than 11,000 in 2020.

The city has a full time police chief, two sergeants, a detective, nine patrol officers, one school resource officer, and three reserve officers. Officers patrol the city twenty-four hours a day, every day.

This wasn't the case in 1933. When residents called the police, they were likely routed to a dispatch office for the County of Clackamas. Constable W.G. Duncan was a one-man police department, only able to respond to complaints within the small confines of the city limits.

He was certainly aware of what was happening at the Flatau farm, but did not have the manpower to handle the situation.

Duncan was not just the constable, but a volunteer firefighter, as well. According to family members who were interviewed for a story in the *Sandy Post*, he was also known to deliver mail on occasion and serve as a janitor for the school.

He died on January 24, 1934, in his role as a volunteer firefighter. He was pulled under the fire engine when his long, white coat (standard firefighting attire at the time), got caught in the wheel of the truck.

GEORGE GUNDERSON

Even though Sandy, Oregon, has grown quite a bit, much of it is rural. Many of the families who lived here in the 1930s are still around, and some remember the people involved in the Flatau incident.

I grew up about seven miles to the northwest of Sandy, in the very small community of Boring. (Yes, that's the real name of the town.) One of my favorite childhood memories was going to Meier Dairy with dad to pick up our milk (in glass bottles!). The dairy was just up the street, so it shouldn't have been a long errand, but my dad would always take the time to visit with the brothers who owned the dairy, Larry and Earl Meier, or their sons Gale, Ken, and Curt, as well as an employee, John Roth. What should have been a fifteen-minute errand would take twice as long. That was fine with me. I'd peer through the windows and watch the Brown Swiss cows lined up in the milking stalls. I'd listen to the loud swishing sound of the milking machines attached to the cows' teats. I'd breathe in the smell of hay and manure, which isn't as bad as one might expect. To this day, whenever I walk into a barn at a fair, I'm taken back to those trips to the dairy with my dad.

The Meier families were our neighbors and we knew them well.

The summer before his senior year in high school, my husband began working for Gale Meier and his wife Sharon at their grocery store, Sharon's Pantry, in Sandy. It was a small store, and he had the opportunity to do a lot of different jobs. He'd work at night "throwing freight" and stocking shelves. He'd work after school bagging groceries at the check stands. He'd work on the weekends in the produce section. He learned a lot, especially about customer service. He got to know my aunt, as she was the bookkeeper for the store. Little did he know then that she would one day be his aunt, too -- by marriage.

I took the time to talk with Gale and Sharon about George Gunderson, who was Sharon's uncle.

George, the son of Norwegian immigrants, Arne and Oline Gunderson, was thirty-six years old when he married nineteen-year-old Bertha Nasshahn in 1930. Bertha's mother and paternal grandparents were immigrants from Germany. Bertha gave birth to twins, Kenneth and Glenna, in 1935, two years after the Flatau incident. They were George and Bertha's only children.

Sharon recalls her uncle being quite nice. He was tall and slim, an avid hunter who was familiar with different types of guns and knew how to use them. One would imagine that neighbor Edward Flatau was aware of George's marksmanship.

Her memory of George's wife Bertha was not as complimentary. She remembered her aunt being somewhat cantankerous and a hoarder. Between the two, Bertha was far more assertive than George.

George passed away in 1970 at the age of seventy-six. After his death, Bertha continued to live on their property until she passed away in 1988. She was also seventy-six at the time of her death.

The Gunderson's property bordered my in-laws' property on the west side, just across the creek. My husband remembers Mrs. Gunderson as being eccentric. He could see her through the trees walking out of her house in a long pioneer-style dress to draw water from the well in the early 1970s, even though her home had running water. He also recalls the bridge where George Gunderson encountered Edward Flatau, although it was almost rotted away when he played down at the creek as a young boy. Time completely destroyed the bridge years ago. The Millers' well house still stands. The family that owned the Millers' property in the 1970s showed my husband the charred wood inside, under the newer siding.

The Millers' well house as it is today.
Photo by Christopher Smith.

Chapter Five
Iowa, Illinois & Indiana - Saturday, April 15, 1933

Aunt Elisabeth's idea of spending the night was actually more like grabbing a few hours of sleep. Mildred wanted to continue her letter to Frances as the trio left Grand Island, but it was too dark at 3 a.m. to see to write. Writing made her feel closer to Frances and her home in Sandy with the tall, green fir trees and majestic Mt. Hood in view. It was a beautiful place just like a picture postcard. Mildred wondered what the kids at school were doing. She hoped they'd stopped talking about her family and the horrible things her father did. Mildred had been mortified by all the talk, but Frances vacillated between anger and indifference. When Frances was angry, she reminded her of their father. She much preferred it when Frances shrugged all the talk off as not caring what "those people" thought. Mildred understood their family tragedy would be a topic of discussion for a long time. After all, her father's capture was like something you'd hear on the radio.

Friday, March 17, 1933

Sandy Ridge - 8:45 a.m.

Amid the chaos of the fire, Edward had been able to avoid detection by the police as he maneuvered from the creek back to his farm. He could see what appeared to be police cars down by the road. He knew his only chance was to hide in the nearest outbuilding – a chicken coop on the edge of his property. He was going to have to shoot his way out of the situation.

Three of the police officers were unaware of how close they were to Edward until they heard his pistol discharge and the bullets whizzing by their heads. They dropped to the ground and lay still.

Edward sat huddled in the chicken coop, replaying the events of the morning. He knew he'd killed Mabel and likely Anna. He'd set his cousin's home on fire and taken shots at police. He decided that if this was going to end, it would be the way it started: on his terms. He placed his revolver in his mouth and pulled the trigger.

Police heard a muffled gun shot and moved in. They found Edward in the rear of the chicken coop, writhing in pain. Still believing he was in control, Edward moved his pistol from one hand to the other and feebly aimed it at them. With Officer Watkins covering him, Officer Snow charged and stepped on Edward's wrist, pinning both hand and gun to the ground. The incident was over.

The officers examined Edward and discovered that he had fired the pistol through the roof of his mouth in an attempted suicide. The bullet penetrated through the skull and lodged beneath the scalp on the crown of his head.

"Ready for breakfast, Mildred?" asked Uncle August as they pulled into Blair, Nebraska. Mildred was glad for the small talk over breakfast. She didn't care that Blair was the last town they'd pass through in Nebraska before entering Iowa or that they'd soon be crossing the Missouri River. However, even listening to Uncle August and Aunt Elisabeth talk about the itinerary for the day was better than reliving her memories.

When they got back on the road, there was enough daylight for Mildred to resume writing her letter to Frances.

We crossed the Missouri River on a huge bridge. They make you pay a toll to cross. It's a pretty dirty river! We've come across a lot of streams and lakes with ducks swimming in them. We are making good time. We're in Iowa, and then we go through Illinois and the tip of Indiana before entering Michigan. I've seen a lot of

things and I'm getting to know Uncle August and
Aunt Elisabeth. I can't wait for you to visit us,
Frances.

Mildred stopped writing and pondered her last sentence. Frances was truly the only one who came close to understanding what she felt. Although Frances hadn't been at the farm to witness the terrifying events, she understood the loss of their mother and Mabel. Frances blamed herself for not being there. Frances had inherited Edward's temper, and was sure she could have done something to stop him. Mildred didn't believe it would have made a difference. In fact, Mildred believed she would be mourning the loss of two sisters instead of one if Frances had been there. Frances was a fighter, and that trait was necessary given the circumstances she was battling back in Portland.

I'm so sorry you had to stay behind and
deal with all the legal stuff. I still can't believe
how that one lawyer tried to keep us from
getting anything from the sale of the farm. I'm
glad you're there finishing all the things that
need to be finished, but I am lonely without you.

So many things were hard for Mildred to understand. Why would a lawyer try to keep two young girls from having the money from the sale of the farm? Sure, the house wasn't as nice as some – how did the newspaper describe it? Oh, yes, "small" and "dilapidated." It was embarrassing to know their private family life was laid out for all to read. The Flataus "fought all the time," neighbors had told the reporter. She guessed it was silly to think neighbors were unaware of the family's troubles, yet she was surprised at just how transparent her family life was – even behind closed doors.

> *Have you talked to the Millers? It was so*
> *nice of them to come to the hospital and stay*
> *with us until...*

Mildred couldn't finish the sentence. It was still so hard to accept that her mother had died. She tried to think of something else, but the scene from the hospital at her mother's bedside continued to replay in her mind.

Friday, March 17, 1933
The Longest and Shortest Seven Hours
9:30 a.m. – Oregon City

The drive to Hutchinson General Hospital in Oregon City took barely thirty minutes, but seemed to take hours. Mildred clenched and unclenched her hands in her lap. She glanced back at her mother, who would lapse between consciousness and unconsciousness. The only way Mildred could tell the difference was by her mother's groaning. Her mother's face was so pale. The doctor in Sandy had done what he could to stop the bleeding, but it wasn't working. He'd also done what he could to wrap up Mabel's body so it would not cause Anna or Mildred further distress.

Mr. Anderson pulled onto a side road, and Mildred could see the hospital up ahead.

"We're here, Mother," said Mildred. "We're at the hospital. They'll take care of you. Everything will be alright, Mother."

Hospital attendants dressed in white shirts and trousers rushed to meet the car. They carefully removed Anna from the back seat of Mr. Anderson's car and quickly took her through the emergency room doors. Mildred started to follow, but was stopped by a tall gentleman in a dark blue suit.

"Are you Mildred Flatau," asked the gentleman.

"Yes, sir," replied Mildred.

"Please wait here for a moment," he said, while walking past her toward Mr. Anderson.

Mr. Anderson and the gentleman talked briefly, and then the gentleman returned to Mildred.

"Follow me, Miss Flatau," instructed the gentleman.

Mildred obeyed, but glanced back just in time to notice a black car pulling in behind Mr. Anderson's car. Mildred recognized the car as a hearse. Once more the tragedy of the day hit her. The hearse was there to take her little sister Mabel away. She swallowed hard.

Mildred continued to follow the gentleman to a small office where deputy sheriffs were waiting for her.

"Officers, this is Mildred Flatau. Let me know if you need anything," said the gentleman as he turned to walk away.

"We know this is a terrible time for you," said one of the officers as he rose from his seat to close the door. "We need you to give us a statement of what happened. That will help us a great deal, Miss Flatau."

Mildred knew this was necessary and she wanted to do it. She wanted the police to know exactly what her father had done.

She sat down, took a deep breath and provided a detailed account of what had happened that morning. The police were shocked that she had been able to talk her father out of shooting her as well. Mildred knew it was a miracle.

When Mildred was done, the officers took her to the hospital waiting room. Herman, Ida, and Otto Miller had arrived. Ida walked to Mildred and hugged her tightly.

"Everything is going to be alright, dear," Ida said in a soothing voice.

"Frances," uttered Mildred. "Does Frances know?"

"I think Paul Buuck was going to call her," offered Otto.

The doctor came out of Anna's room. "I'm really sorry, but there's nothing we can do. It's just a matter of time before she succumbs to her injuries."

Ida held Mildred tighter and cried. Mildred wasn't able to shed a tear.

"Your father was brought in a few minutes ago," continued the doctor. "He may survive."

"My father," asked Mildred unaware that her father had shot himself.

Herman Miller started to explain what had happened after Mildred had left the farm seeking help for her mother, but stopped when he saw Frances walk in.

"I should have been there," declared Frances as she embraced Mildred. "I could have stopped it."

Mildred objected, "No, Frances. If you'd been there you might be dead, too. Did you know father is here, too?"

Frances looked puzzled.

"Before the police could arrest your father, he shot himself," explained Herman Miller.

The two sisters fell silent, not knowing what to say to each other. Their little sister Mabel was dead. Their mother was dying. Their father had shot himself but may live. That was almost more than they could take.

The doctor came back to the waiting room and suggested they say goodbye to their mother. He couldn't predict how much longer she'd live.

They walked into their mother's hospital room. It wasn't even really a room, but a back portion of the emergency room sectioned off with curtains. Frances looked as pale as their mother. Mildred had never seen Frances look weak. It was unsettling. Frances breathed deeply and took her mother's hand. It was cold to the touch. She swallowed hard, avoiding tears.

"Mother would want us to pray," Frances said flatly.

Both girls bowed their heads, but said no words. Mildred couldn't remember what they were supposed to pray when someone was sick or dying. After a long pause, Frances said, "Amen."

Mildred didn't ask if Frances remembered the prayers. It didn't matter.

They looked at their unconscious mother, said goodbye, and left the room.

The girls walked back to the waiting room and listened as the Millers tried to make small talk.

Mildred looked around the room. Everything was white. The walls were white. The floors were white. It smelled strongly of antiseptic. If the color white had a smell, Mildred was sure this must be what it smelled like. The chairs were metal with green padded vinyl seats, but that was the only thing that wasn't white.

The Millers sat with Mildred and Frances until Anna passed away about seven hours after she had been shot. That she had not died at the farm was amazing. It was a long, agonizing seven hours, but yet it was over too soon.

Frances decided Mildred would stay with her for the weekend. It would give them both someone to lean on as they tried to come to terms with what had happened. Besides, they would have many decisions to make over the next few days. However, Frances was well aware that Mildred would need to finish out the school year. She should do that at her school in Sandy, not a new school in Portland.

"I'll take Mildred home with me for the weekend, but would it be possible for her to stay with you to finish out the school year?" Frances asked the Millers.

Ida and Herman looked at each other. They had not wanted the girls to learn of their own devastation while mourning the loss of their mother and sister.

Herman cleared his throat and began to tell Frances and Mildred about their father burning the Millers' house.

Mildred and Frances were stunned. Mildred remembered seeing her father trudge across the field toward the Miller's home. They had not escaped her father's rage. The Millers were suffering a great loss, but didn't say a word in order to protect the girls in their time of grief.

"Mildred would be more than welcome to stay with us, but right now, we're figuring out where we will be staying until we can rebuild our house," explained Herman.

Ida noticed how uncomfortable the girls were hearing the news. "Oh, don't worry about us. Our children will help us, and of course all the people in the church. I'm sure the neighbors will help, too. We'll be fine."

Mildred walked with Frances to the hospital parking lot. Her mind was whirling with the events of the day. Mabel was dead. Her mother was dead. The only relatives she knew well, the Millers, had lost their home. She couldn't live with them and finish out the school year. Frances really didn't have room for her, either.

"Frances, what are we going to do?" asked Mildred.

"We're going to go to my house, eat something, then go to sleep," replied Frances. "Tomorrow we'll call Aunt Elisabeth in Detroit."

"But what about…"

Frances cut off Mildred, "We're not going to discuss things we can't figure out tonight. Don't worry about your dress. We can wash it when we get home."

Mildred looked down at her dress that she'd been so happy to put on that morning and for the first time noticed it was speckled with blood.

Mildred was only vaguely aware that not only had they left Nebraska, but they were nearly through Iowa. Reliving her mother's last hours was painful, and even more so when she considered that her father lived a full week until his self-inflicted gunshot wound finally ended his life. Why couldn't he have died sooner and her mother lasted longer? The Millers had been so kind to them, and even to her father. How could they visit him in the hospital after what he did to their home?

She was grateful that the neighbors had worked together to help the Millers salvage what they could after the fire. The house had been reduced to a heap of ash, but the farm buildings had been spared. Mildred still found it hard to believe that her father was capable of so much violence and hatred to those outside of their immediate family. She had seen and heard him act violently with her mother and, to be honest, her mother seemed to provoke him. But what had the Millers done to deserve his rage?

The newspaper reported that her father had "nursed a deep enmity against the Millers for years." She knew they hadn't spoken for years, so why couldn't he just leave them alone? They had nothing to do with her parents' argument that had started the whole terrible chain of events of that day. Could it really be just as simple as the newspaper account surmised?

"The opinion among neighbors indicated that Flatau's hatred was born of a deep envy. The picturesque farm house, as typical as something from an agricultural advertisement, the neat yard and fields and the well-stocked barn rankled in Flatau's gaze whenever he looked at them. His own place is a study of rural decadence and disarray. This, neighbors thought, coupled with the fact that his farm and home were mortgaged and his well declared unsanitary recently by a state inspector, led to the outbreak."

All this horrific carnage because her father had fallen on hard times and was jealous of his cousin and her husband's success?

Mildred decided to erase the last unfinished sentence and begin the paragraph again.

Have you talked to the Millers? Have they started building their new house? I hope they're not mad at us.

"Mildred," said Aunt Elisabeth, "we don't want to try to follow the maps and road signs after dark, so help us look for a place to spend the night."

"Where are we?" asked Mildred.

Uncle August answered quickly, "Indiana!"

"Yes, we're in Indiana," confirmed Aunt Elisabeth, "but we're not sure exactly where in Indiana."

If her father had been lost while driving, she was sure he would have been upset and blamed her mother, and she supposed her mother would've escalated things by saying something to further annoy him. Instead of anger and blame, Mildred noticed just simple understanding between Uncle August and Aunt Elisabeth. It was going to take some time to get used to the difference.

Tomorrow, Sunday, they'd arrive in Detroit, Michigan, and on Monday she would begin a new life in a new school with new friends. No one would know about the fights between her father and mother. No one would know her family was about to lose their farm. Most importantly, no one would know how her father, mother and sister Mabel died.

Mildred wrote one last paragraph to Frances.

I've been thinking about what you said about keeping what happened a secret. I want to start new in Michigan. I don't want to lie, but

*I don't want to bring all those memories to my
new home. I've been thinking that if anyone asks
we can just say there was a fire and our parents
and sister died. That's true, right, Frances?*

◆ **Secret Kept, Secret Revealed** ◆

Whether Frances asked Mildred to deceive their new
acquaintances regarding the circumstances of their parents' death
and that of their sister Mabel is unknown. However, Frances and
Mildred did keep the story a secret for decades, only mentioning a
fire and the deaths.

After settling her parents' estate, Frances visited Mildred,
Uncle August, and Aunt Elisabeth in Detroit, and was introduced to a
young man who was to become her future husband. She chose to
stay in Detroit.

Frances, Mildred, Aunt Elisabeth, and Uncle August taken in Detroit
in 1937.

Photo courtesy of Evelyn Morgan and Donald Steinhart.

Frances' daughters discovered the truth while the family was living on a farm with Frances' in-laws. The girls were going through some of their mother's "treasures" and found the newspaper article. They mentioned the truth to their mother at a later date (without divulging how they knew), and Frances went into a rage and blamed their paternal grandmother with telling the story. According to her daughter, Evelyn, "It was not a pretty sight, so we kept everything to ourselves."

Evelyn didn't even mention the newspaper article to her Aunt Mildred, with whom she was very close, considering her a mentor and "mother" figure. Mildred did finally share the story with Evelyn, but not until Evelyn was married. Mildred sent a copy of the newspaper article to Evelyn decades later.

Fearing her mother's wrath, Evelyn did not share the true story with her own children until after Frances died from liver cancer about two months before her 76th birthday.

"Mildred told me several times in her later years that she often thought about writing a book about how God delivered her from the hands of the enemy, but she didn't know how to go about it," revealed Evelyn. "Mildred understood she had to be very careful and it would have to wait until her sister was gone. It was her wish for God to be glorified in saving her life."

Mildred shared the story with her husband Gerry before they were married in 1946, but no mention of the incident was made afterward. She and her husband were unable to have children of their own, which is one of the reasons Mildred was so close to her niece, Evelyn.

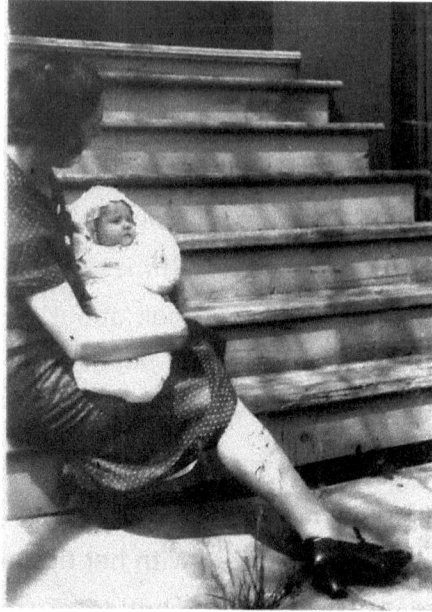

Mildred holding her newborn niece, Evelyn.
Photo courtesy of Evelyn Morgan and Donald Steinhart.

However, in 1960, twenty-seven years after Mildred lived through the horrific incident, a purpose for God sparing her life became evident. In April of that year, a mother of nine children (ages two to fifteen) died of cancer. Her husband was unable to care for all the children, so some were put in foster care and the four youngest were put up for adoption. Gerry and Mildred adopted two of those children, Geraldine and Danell. It's difficult to imagine any other mother being able to identify with the loss these two young girls had experienced as well as Mildred did.

Danell shared her first memories of her new home: "I remember Mom and Dad taking us to church the first time and how proud they were of their 'new' daughters and of their church. Every day before we left for school, we would sit down in the living room and read the Bible and pray with Mom. Without their love, guidance and prayers (lots of them!), I don't believe I would be the person I am today. "

Although Mildred had found a purpose for surviving the violence of her youth, like Frances, she kept the events a secret from her children, as well. Given the secrecy, it's interesting that they and their husbands traveled to Sandy, Oregon, in 1983 – the 50th anniversary of the tragedy. They visited their schoolmate, Alvina Wunische Koenig Rau, and even stopped to visit the property where they'd lived. The old barn was the only remaining building on their childhood property.

The barn built by Edward Flatau and Paul Buuck.
Photo courtesy of Ruth Smith.

Alvina Wunische Koenig Rau with Frances and Alfred Buckstein.
Taken during Frances and Mildred's trip to Oregon in 1983, fifty
years after the incident. Mildred's daughter Danell first heard the
full story of her grandparents' death from Alvina in 1999.
Photo courtesy of Evelyn Morgan

Danell remembers hearing the story for the first time in 1999. "My husband and I happened to be living in Portland and went to visit an old school friend of Mom's (Alvina), who proceeded to tell me how tragic it (the story) was and I just sat there - stunned! I could not believe what I was hearing. I had thought Mom's mother and sister were killed in a fire. We moved back to Michigan in 2000

92

and Mom asked about my meeting with her friend, and added that she guessed I now knew the real story. She brought out the newspaper clippings and I read them. Mom still did not talk about the event, although once in a while she would say something in passing."

Mildred lived life fully to the age of ninety and had no serious illnesses. She was active in her church ministering in the nursery and helping with the annual Vacation Bible School every summer.

Danell and her mother Mildred June 1972 at Danell's high school graduation.

Photo courtesy of Danell Cape Rutherford.

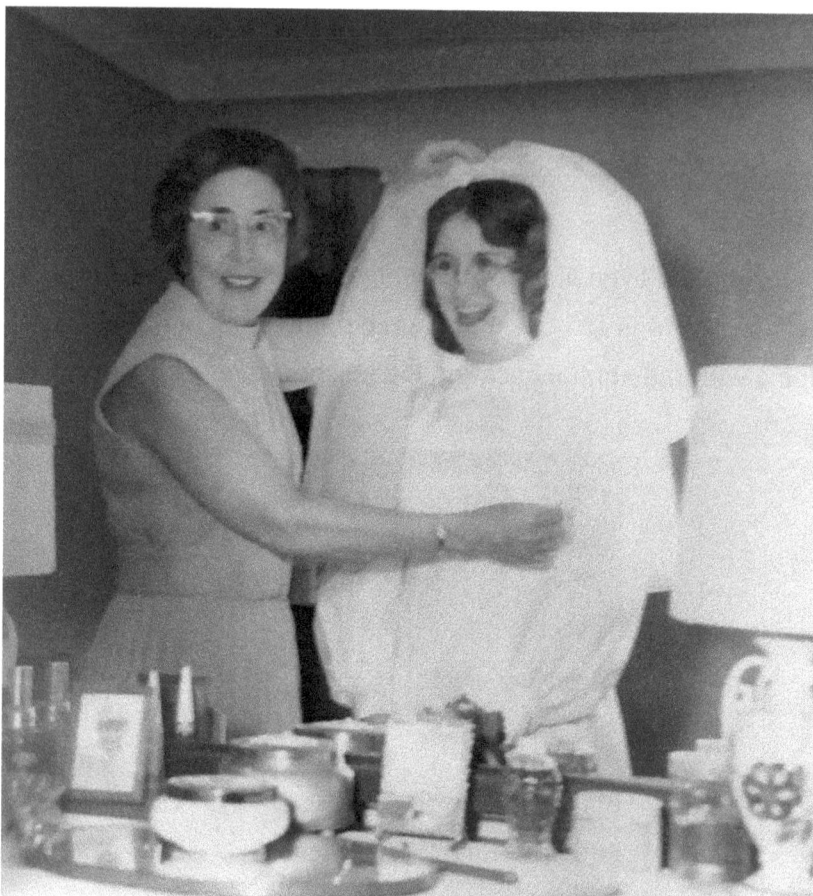

Danell and her mother Mildred on Danell's wedding day,
May 5, 1973. The two photo frames visible on the dresser hold
photos of Mildred's mother Anna and her sister Mabel.
Photo courtesy of Danell Cape Rutherford.

Danell has shared her mother's story and how Mildred lived her life for Christ. "Mom never once used the tragic deaths of her mother and sister to say 'poor me' and use it as an excuse like most

94

people do. If Mom could live her life after witnessing a tragedy like that anyone can."

Danell, Mildred, and Evelyn taken in Detroit about three weeks before Mildred passed away.

Photo courtesy of Danell Cape Rutherford.

Chapter Six

DISCOVERING THE FLATAU FAMILY
COMING TO AMERICA

When Edward Flatau was fifteen years of age, he boarded the *SS Dresden in Bremen, Germany, with his father Daniel, mother Emilia, sister Louisa (eighteen) and brother Emil (thirteen) to sail to the United States. They landed in Baltimore, Maryland on November 17, 1894, with nothing but two suitcases.

Ten years later, on April 9, 1904, at age twenty-five, Anna Weise boarded a ship named the **Graf Waldersee in Cuxhaven, Germany, bound for the United States. The Graf Waldersee arrived in New York City on April 23, 1904. According to the records of the ship, Anna had $30.

In the late 19th and early 20th Century, a transatlantic voyage from Europe to the United States could be made in about a week. Weather conditions could, and did, add to that time.

It is likely that both Edward and Anna traveled in small, cramped steerage or third class cabins as they both passed through immigration inspections at Ellis Island. Passengers traveling in first or second class were not subject to the Ellis Island experience, but instead underwent a cursory inspection aboard ship. The thinking behind that difference was that if a person could afford to purchase a first or second class ticket, they were less likely to become dependent on the government for assistance due to medical or legal reasons.

While it is unclear why Edward's family chose to leave their home in Germany, some common reasons amongst immigrants at the time included: worsening opportunities for farm ownership, persecution of some religious groups, and military conscription. In contrast, the United States offered religious freedom and better economic conditions, especially the opportunity to own land.

It's difficult to assume Anna would have immigrated to the United States by herself for any of the common reasons. According to the research of Anna's family members, she was the first of two members of her immediate family to leave Germany. Her younger sister Elisabeth didn't arrive until 1914 when political unrest would have been underway in Europe. Why would a young woman like Anna leave the security of family and home to come to a new country alone? Perhaps a broken heart?

ONCE IN A LIFETIME TRIP

As we've grown accustomed to the tales of immigration to the United States, we forget the perils of their journey. Because travel has become fairly common for even those of modest means, we underestimate the difficulty of the decision to, in most cases, forever leave behind family, property, and culture.

When our kids were five and nine years of age, my husband and I decided to take them to Walt Disney World for a week. We live in Oregon, so this involved a long plane trip across the country to Orlando, Florida. I booked a red-eye flight, thinking our children would sleep on the plane, which was quite naïve.

We planned for months. I purchased clothing for the kids, my husband, and myself. I researched all the activities in the area and made an itinerary for the Disney parks (Magic Kingdom, Epcot, and MGM) and Universal Studios.

The week before the trip was filled with packing suitcases for each of us, putting together backpacks for the kids and confirming all of our reservations. I made sure we had plenty of film for the camera and backup batteries. The entire house became a staging area for this "once in a lifetime" trip.

We arrived at the airport and anxiously waited to board our flight. I was looking forward to settling into our seats and sleeping until we had to change planes in Dallas, Texas. I tried to sleep. My husband tried to sleep. Neither of our kids followed our example. They were too excited! It was our son's first time on an airplane. It was our daughter's second flight, but she didn't really remember the first time when she was two years old.

We arrived in Orlando, sleep-deprived and hungry, but before we could sleep or eat, we had to pick up the rental car and check into the condominium. The rental car agency was a mad house with a long line of customers. It seemed to take much longer than necessary, but my husband's delightful attitude earned us a nice free upgrade.

We loaded our luggage into the rental car and headed to the grocery store on our way to the condominium. Once we checked into the condo, I fixed a quick breakfast and declared it "bedtime!"

All the kids could do was ask when we were going to the park; after all, it was late morning. They didn't want to waste a single moment of the trip napping.

We had a fun time while we were in Orlando. However, getting there and returning was pretty stressful, and I considered that a difficult trip. In comparison to the journey immigrants have taken to reach the United States though, our little vacation was figuratively, and literally, a walk in the park.

* The SS Dresden was built in Glasgow, Scotland, and launched December 1, 1889. The Norddeutscher Lloyd Company of Bremen, Germany, had ordered eight passenger-cargo ships of the same type built, and the Dresden was the first of these eight ships to be completed. The Dresden was sold three times before being sunk by a Russian destroyer in the Black Sea on November 6, 1914.

**The Graf Waldersee was a passenger liner built in 1898 by Blohm & Voss in Hamburg, Germany for the Hamburg America Line's Hamburg to New York service. She was launched originally with 4 masts but reduced to two within a few years. The ship was out of service for the duration of World War 1 and was handed over to the United States in 1919 for use as a transport ship. A year later she was transferred to the British government before being scraped in Hamburg in 1922.

EDWARD FRIEDRICH FLATAU

Edward Flatau: Taken at his sister Louisa's wedding, May 13, 1898, in Perham, Otter Tail, Minnesota, United States.
Photo and information courtesy of Martha Laird, granddaughter of Albert and Louisa (Flatau) Weise, and the late Reginald "Roman" Smith, grandnephew of Albert Weise.

Edward Friedrich Flatau was born on April 5, 1879, in Rosenfelde, Schleswig-Holstein, Germany. After sailing to the United States, he and his family continued their journey from the East Coast to their new home in Fairchild, Wisconsin, to live with Edward's mother's family, the Neumanns. The decision to leave Germany may have been easier due to extended family already living in the United States. Immigration records show most of Edward's half-siblings from his father's first marriage had already arrived in the United States prior to 1894.

Census records show Edward's family settling in Hobart Township, Otter Tail County, Minnesota, by 1900. Edward was still living in Hobart when the Minnesota census was taken in 1905. It appears that Edward's family were not the only members of the Flatau family to make Otter Tail County their home. Flatau Cemetery, the resting place of forty-three members of the Flatau family, including Edward's parents, is located within that county.

The 1910 census indicates that Edward, age thirty-one had moved to the area of Sandy, Oregon. His occupation is listed as the "sawmill industry," but he is listed as unemployed. Several members of Edward's family appear to have migrated to Sandy, Oregon, around the same time, including his cousins, Herman C. Miller and Ida Flatau Miller and his nephew Theodore F. Flatau. They are all located in the same neighborhood in the 1910 census.

ANNA WEISE FLATAU

Anna Weise: Taken in early 1900s, perhaps in Germany before she left for the United States.

Photo and information courtesy of Evelyn Morgan & Donald Steinhart.

Anna Hedwig Weise was born on April 4, 1879, in Bischofswerda, Saxony, Germany to Karl Fredrich Robert Weise and Minna Hedwig Fischer Weise. She was the third of nine children.

Weise family portrait: Taken in Germany, late 1890s.
L-R: Edith, Richard, Father (sitting), Fred, Elisabeth, Rudolf, Mother (sitting), Paul, Anna.
Photo and information courtesy of Evelyn Morgan & Donald Steinhart.

Anna appears in the 1910 census as living in Portland, Oregon, where she was employed as a maid. How she came to be living on the opposite coast from which she landed after her arrival from Germany is a mystery.

THEIR LIFE TOGETHER

Edward Flatau married Anna Weise on May 22, 1910, in Sandy, Oregon, at the Immanuel Lutheran Church. How Anna and Edward met is unclear. They were both thirty-one years of age, and it appears this was a first marriage for both. As they were older, it's quite possible that this was an arranged marriage, but I have not found evidence of this.

Edward's sister, Louisa, married into the Weise family, but her husband was not a sibling of Anna. Weise is a common German surname, so it's quite possible there's no family relationship. Edward's family lived in the north central part of Germany, near Denmark, and Anna's family lived in the eastern part of Germany near the borders of Poland and Czechoslovakia – about 350 miles apart.

Even though Sandy is only about thirty-five miles southeast of Portland, it's not likely they would have just "bumped into one another." It's possible that they met through some sort of involvement in the Lutheran churches of the area.

They began their married life on the farm Edward had purchased in Sandy, Oregon.

They had three daughters during their marriage: Frances (October 26, 1913), Mildred (April 4, 1917), and Mabel (October 27, 1921). All three were baptized at the same Lutheran church in which their parents were married.

Anna, Frances, and Mildred Flatau: Taken in Sandy, Oregon about 1920.

Photo and information courtesy of Evelyn Morgan & Donald Steinhart.

I found it interesting that Edward's Oregon driver's license information shows him living in Boring, Oregon, on September 12, 1918. At that time, he and Anna still owned the farm in Sandy, making me wonder whether he left the family for a period of time.

Other documentation shows him living in Sandy again on September 5, 1919.

Anna and Edward Flatau: Taken in Sandy, Oregon in the early 1930s.

Photo and information courtesy of Evelyn Morgan & Donald Steinhart.

Anna died on March 17, 1933, at Hutchinson General Hospital in Oregon City, Oregon, at the age of fifty-three due to gunshots inflicted by Edward. She is buried next to her daughter Mabel in Rose

City Cemetery in Portland, Oregon. Their graves are unmarked. According to cemetery records, the two graves were purchased by Frances for $74. She financed the purchase, which she paid off in six monthly installments. I was surprised Frances chose to have her mother and sister buried in Portland rather than their hometown of Sandy. However, at the time, Frances lived less than a mile from Rose City Cemetery, so it was likely she wanted them close by.

Entrance to Rose City Cemetery, and the location of Anna and Mabel's graves.

Photo by Linda D'Ae-Smith.

On March 24, 1933, one week after the incident, a grand jury returned three indictments against Edward; two counts of murder in the first degree and one count of arson.

Edward died one day later on March 25, 1933, at Hutchinson General Hospital in Oregon City, Oregon, at the age of fifty-three. He had survived eight days after he shot himself in an attempted suicide. His remains were taken to Oregon City Funeral Home.

Edward is buried in the "potter's field" area of Mt. View Cemetery in Oregon City. The cemetery has no record of his burial: however, the Oregon City Historical Society and the Oregon City Funeral Home concur that Mt. View Cemetery is his resting place.

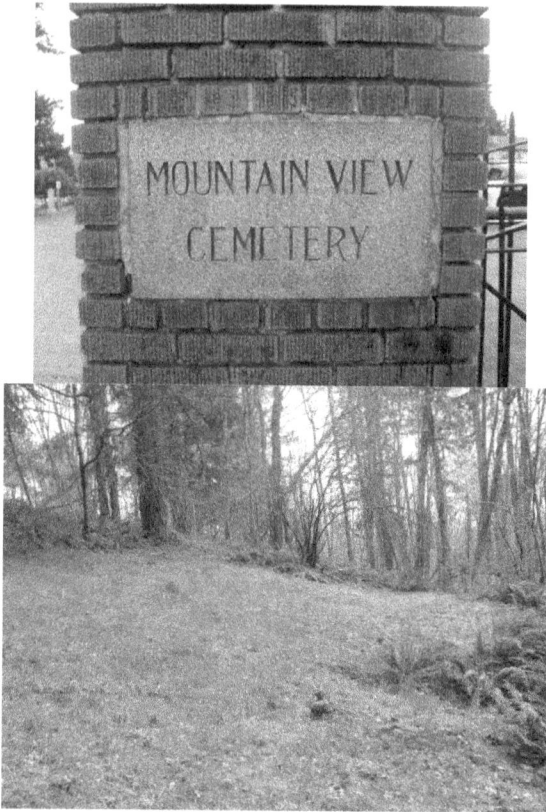

Entrance to Mountain View Cemetery and the "potter's field" area. Most graves are unmarked in this section. He was buried at the expense of the State of Oregon, which was later reimbursed by the proceeds of his estate.

Photo by Linda D'Ae-Smith.

SISTERS

While tragedy can drive family apart, it seems to have created a special protective and enduring bond between these two Flatau sisters.

Frances and Mildred's family shared a little about that sister relationship, and it sounds very much like my mother and aunt.

My mother and her sister, who is three years younger, have always been extremely close. I remember them talking or visiting in person almost every day during my childhood.

Aunt Sherry lived less than ten miles from us when I was very young, and I recall she and my mother getting together to give each other "perms." I can still smell those foul chemicals. They had vanity cases filled with the different colored rods that determined the tightness of the curls.

We'd head to Aunt Sherry's so she and my mom could shop for groceries together. My older siblings were school-aged, so I would get to spend the day with my "bookend" cousins; Jimmy is nine months older than I and Debbie is eight months younger. I'm sure it would have been easier for my mom to just take me to the store, but I think she felt sorry for Aunt Sherry having to wrangle two little kids so close in age.

A whole new dimension opened up for these two sisters when Aunt Sherry's family moved and we became neighbors. They spent even more time together, and amazingly, they remained close. Even today, they talk several times a week.

I completely understood when Frances' daughter Evelyn shared the following about her mother and aunt; "They got together as much as possible and had healthy gab fests."

Upon learning about two little girls in her community who were going to be put up for adoption, it was Frances who suggested Mildred adopt the girls.

Frances and Mildred Flatau – 1917.

Photo and Information provided by Evelyn Morgan and Donald Steinhart.

Frances and Mildred Flatau – 1918.
Photo and information provided by Evelyn Morgan and Donald Steinhart.

FRANCES REGINA HEDWIG FLATAU

Frances Flatau – 1931: Possibly a high school graduation photo.
Photo and information provided of Evelyn Morgan and Donald
Steinhart.

Frances Regina Hedwig Flatau was born on October 26, 1913, in Sandy, Oregon. After graduating from high school, she went to work in Portland as a maid, a step common among her peers.

She was living in Portland when her father Edward murdered her mother Anna and sister Mabel. Legal documents reveal that Frances took charge of her father's estate for the benefit of Mildred.

On April 6, 1933, not quite three weeks after her father's rampage, The Portland Sanitarium and Benevolent Association petitioned the court as a principal creditor of the decedent (Edward) to have their representative, J.S. Donaldson, appointed administrator of the estate. The Portland Sanitarium and Benevolent Association stated in their petition that "...said decedent left an estate consisting of real and personal property of the probable value of $350; that it is doubtful if the real property can be rented and, therefore, your petitioner alleges that it has only a nominal rental value."

The honorable Earl C. Latourette granted the petitioner's request, but Frances fought back. Eight days later, on April 14, 1933, J.S. Donaldson tendered his resignation as administrator of the estate valued at $800 in personal property and $3,500 in real property, with a probable yearly rental value of $150.

According to her family, Frances had had "definite trust issues that seemed odd." She was not in favor of selling her husband's family farm, even though they were "better off for it in the long run." This revelation of her early experience with land and lawyers explains why Frances had trust issues with legal matters and real estate transactions.

The final distribution of Edward's estate was quite small. He had refinanced the land several times over and owed many creditors. However, in the end, more than two years later on April 25, 1935, Frances was awarded $45.93 cash and the paper on the second mortgage, with a balance of $718.18 "for the support, nurture and education of Mildred Flatau."

At some point after the settlement of the estate, Frances went to visit Mildred in Michigan. She never returned to live in Oregon. Her Uncle August introduced her to Gustave Alfred Buckstein and they married on June 5, 1937

Wedding photo of Alfred and Frances Buckstein: L-R: Howard Ziehl, Edna (Buckstein) Ziehl, Frances (Flatau) Buckstein, Alfred Buckstein, Mildred Flatau, unknown attendant– Detroit, Michigan.
Photo and information provided of Evelyn Morgan and Donald Steinhart.

In July of 1989, Frances and Alfred traveled from Michigan to North Carolina for their grandson's wedding. Shortly after they returned home, Frances was diagnosed with cancer. She died on August 26 at the age of seventy-five.

Alfred and Frances Buckstein on his family farm
where they lived the majority of their married lives.
Photo and information provided of Evelyn Morgan and Donald Steinhart.

119

MILDRED ELISABETH FLATAU

Mildred Elisabeth Flatau – possibly 1935.
Photo and information provided of Evelyn Morgan and Donald Steinhart.

Mildred Elisabeth Flatau was born on April 4, 1917, in Sandy, Oregon, which happened to be her mother's 38th birthday.

After the death of her parents in 1933, she went to live in Detroit, Michigan, with her Uncle August and Aunt Elisabeth, who was her mother's sister.

August Meyer, Mildred Flatau, and Elisabeth Meyer.
Photo provided of Evelyn Morgan and Donald Steinhart.

August and Elisabeth were very involved at Ebenezer Baptist Church (German Baptist) and Mildred became involved as well. While attending the church, Mildred became acquainted with another congregant, Gerald Cape, who had been discharged from the Army. They married on October 5, 1946.

Gerald and Mildred Cape's wedding: Frances and Alfred Buckstein are on the far left.
Photo and information provided of Evelyn Morgan and Donald Steinhart.

Mildred and Gerry were very active in the church. Mildred was a Sunday School teacher and Gerry was a deacon. They had an "open door policy" and entertained many ministers, special speakers, and musical groups who were invited to the church.

Mildred and Gerry were unable to have children, so when Frances suggested they adopt two little girls whose mother had recently passed away, they did so without hesitation. Mildred's Uncle August had died in 1947, long before the girls were adopted, or born for that matter, but Aunt Elisabeth became known as their grandmother.

In addition to their church life, Mildred and Gerry enjoyed long vacations every summer to various parts of the country.

Mildred and Gerry vacationing in Bonne Terre, MO, September 1956.
Photo and information provided of Evelyn Morgan and Donald Steinhart.

Gerry and Mildred Cape, 50th Wedding Anniversary, 1996.

Photo and information provided by Evelyn Morgan

Gerry and Mildred Cape, 60th Wedding Anniversary, 2006.
Photo and information provided by Evelyn Morgan.

Mildred also had a profound impact on her niece Evelyn, Frances' daughter. She fondly recalls enjoying Sunday afternoon sightseeing rides around Detroit and Mildred driving her from Detroit to Illinois to attend Wheaton College. She was unable to attend her Aunt Mildred's 90th birthday celebration, but visited a few months later.

"We had a wonderful time. I asked her what she would like to do with me. She wanted to take a ride to see all the places in Detroit that meant anything to her, so we did. Mind you, at 90, she was my tour guide and told me every turn I was to make for about four hours. We ended the trip with a stop at Dairy Queen - a special treat. What a glorious day I will never forget, and so timely. Three weeks later, we had to return to Detroit for her funeral.

Mildred's daughter Danell and her sister were with Mildred when she left this world on October 11, 2007.

"My sister and I were with Mom when she died. I had never watched someone die before. Mom had a lot of wrinkles, but as she lay there dying you could see the wrinkles going away. She looked so much younger."

Chapter Seven

DOMESTIC VIOLENCE; MY DAUGHTER AND MILDERD

Our daughter left home at age nineteen to join the armed forces. Things appeared to be going well for her while she was in basic training, and we were happy to have her home for the holidays before she headed to "A School" to learn about her job in the military. However, once she arrived at her training location, we stopped hearing from her.

Panic sets in pretty quickly when your oldest child leaves home and stops communicating. Even as teens, when they start gaining more control over their lives, as is normal and healthy, you still have a pretty good idea of where they are at any given point in the day (even if you don't know what they are doing). Not knowing was completely new territory and we were concerned.

We finally learned that the reason for her silence was a new boyfriend. There was plenty of reason to keep this boyfriend a secret, and the red flags began to show, if subtly. We were quite relieved that after graduation, her orders sent her to the East Coast, far away from her boyfriend.

Our relief was short-lived, however, when we discovered she'd secretly married her boyfriend. Unbeknownst to us, we were on a journey of observing our daughter in a domestic violence situation. Red flags now were popping up regularly, but we had no idea what to do or how to help our daughter. This was made more difficult by the fact that she wanted us to know what was going on, but absolutely did not want help or advice. The distance of thousands of miles separating us from her made us feel helpless.

I finally called the local National Domestic Violence Hotline. They were very patient, didn't ask revealing questions, and suggested that we review a checklist to discover whether our daughter was in danger.

When I got the checklist, I was terrified for my daughter. Eleven of the fifteen signs below checked off in my daughter's situation. My husband and I talked about what we could and couldn't do. We agreed that we could share that what she was encountering was domestic violence, but we could not force her to accept the information.

My husband was better at just allowing our daughter to digest the information. I wasn't as patient, but eventually, I had no options but to let her figure things out on her own.

I got a phone call one evening and recognized the name on the Caller ID as someone with whom my daughter had been stationed. I answered the call and my daughter was on the line. She told me her husband had shut her phone off, so she couldn't use it. (RED FLAG!) I thought this might be a turning point, but no. I got another phone call from my daughter informing me that her husband had cheated on her. Again, I thought this would cause her to walk away. I was wrong.

My daughter asked me to fly to the East Coast to meet up with her. It was very last minute, but I made arrangements for time off work and a last minute flight. I hoped I would be able to help her make the decision to leave this unhealthy, toxic, dangerous marriage, but again no.

I was mentally and emotionally exhausted by the situation. Our son was entering his final year of high school and I really needed to be present for all the activities associated with his senior year. We basically told our daughter that we loved her and would always be there for her, but that we would not continue on this roller coaster ride any longer.

I sent our daughter's chaplain all the information and emails we had received and asked him to take over. I later learned that he had done nothing with the information.

Several months had passed when we got a phone call while we were eating dinner. It was our daughter. Her husband had become physically violent and the evidence of that encounter was noticed by her command. This incident gave her cover to ask the military to separate them.

This is not the end of the story, but it was the beginning of her understanding that her situation was a case of domestic violence. She has emotional scars, but is safe and successful.

There's a lot to this story that I cannot share as it would intrude on my daughter's privacy. However, she did give me permission to share what I have written in the hope it might prove helpful to someone in a similar situation.

Mildred's mother experienced domestic violence before the situation turned deadly. The first sign on the list below is "Tells you that you can never do anything right." This seemed to be a common theme for Edward as he berated his wife. Other signs included: he kept her and the girls from attending church or visiting with the Miller family; he insulted, demeaned and shamed Anna with put downs; and he controlled the finances, or lack thereof. Who knows how many other signs he checked off? Obviously, this led to a horrific conclusion, as it too often does.

If in reading this book, you see yourself in Anna, or my daughter, please review the information listed below. Seek help. Seek safety. You are not alone.

WARNING SIGNS OF DOMESTIC VIOLENCE

It's not always easy to tell at the beginning of a relationship if it will become abusive.

In fact, many abusive partners may seem absolutely perfect in the early stages of a relationship. Possessive and controlling behaviors don't always appear overnight, but rather emerge and intensify as the relationship grows.

Domestic violence doesn't look the same in every relationship because every relationship is different. But one thing most abusive relationships have in common is that the abusive partner does many different kinds of things to have more power and control over their partner.

Some of the signs of an abusive relationship include a partner who:

- Tells you that you can never do anything right
- Shows extreme jealousy of your friends and time spent away
- Keeps you or discourages you from seeing friends or family members
- Insults, demeans or shames you with put-downs
- Controls every penny spent in the household
- Takes your money or refuses to give you money for necessary expenses
- Looks at you or acts in ways that scare you
- Controls who you see, where you go, or what you do
- Prevents you from making your own decisions
- Tells you that you are a bad parent or threatens to harm or take away your children
- Prevents you from working or attending school
- Destroys your property or threatens to hurt or kill your pets
- Intimidates you with guns, knives, or other weapons
- Pressures you to have sex when you don't want to or does things sexually you're not comfortable with
- Pressures you to use drugs or alcohol

Reprinted with permission of the National Domestic Violence Hotline

Auxiliary Information

1. **Mildred's Statement to Police**
2. **Mildred's Diary**

Statement of Mildred Elisabeth Flatau:

Oregon City, Oregon,
March 17, 1933

I, Mildred Elisabeth Flatau make the following statement:

At 7:30 a.m. this date, my father, Edward Flatau and my mother Anna Flatau had a dispute relative to my mother leaving for Portland. We had been selling milk in Portland and had recently been degraded, and due to the degradation of our milk contract, we were going to move the separator up to the milk house and sell sour cream. Father has been very slow in accomplishing this task, and mother had reprimanded my father on several occasions for this negligence. This morning my mother again requested him to move the separator and this made my father very angry and he then alluded (sic) to many things that had happened to their lives in the past 21 years. Father called my mother several profane names and then mother went upstairs to pack her things. I got out her suitcase and together we packed. While we were packing, my father came upstairs twice, both times my mother told him to leave. He then told my mother to go ahead and leave and that it would have been better had she left 21 years before. My mother, myself and my sister Mabel then came downstairs; in the meantime my father had obtained a gun which he kept in a dresser drawer down stairs. My father and mother resumed their quarrel and mother attempted to leave the house by the front door, but was stopped by my father. My mother, sister and myself then left the house by way of the back door. Father then left the house by the way of the front door and came around to the back and without saying anything, shot mother in the mouth, then turned to my sister Mabel and shot her through the head. My father then came to me and I grabbed his arm. I then said to him, "Christ is watching you. You cannot do this." And he answered, "I cannot help myself, I am a murderer." I then said to him, "I pray you don't shoot me." My mother then picked up my sister Mabel and laid her upon her back and then mother ran out to the road, my father following her. When they reach the gate my father again shot my mother twice, my father then came back to the house and told me to go inside and sit down, that he was going to spare my life and that I should not watch to see where he went. This is the last time I saw my father. I then ran through the house and joined my mother in the road. At this time some neighbors came and took care of my mother. Shooting took place about 8:30 a.m.

Mildred's Diary
(Copied without corrections to grammar, punctuation, or spelling)

Tuesday April 11, 1933

Starting out from Portland. Stopped for gas. Stopped at the cemitary, got our last glimpse of the two graves. Went on to the Columbia River Highway, drove to the Multnomah Falls. Saw that for the last time till we come west again. Drove on. Got about 10 miles on the other side of the Multnomah Falls saw an accident that had happened the night before. It was a truck had run into the fence there & upset. It was a wood truck with wood on it. Was a terrible mess. We didn't stop.

When we got to the view point on the C.R.H.*we stopped to look around. There were to (sic) men there that had come from Indiana. They plan to spend the summer in Ore. We spoke a few words with them, then we drove on again. Drove along the C.R.**from Portland to Umatilla. Made a turn there and went away from the River. Umatilla is after Hood River but that is as far as we followed the River. It rained some going from Portland to Hood River. Got to Hood River it quit. When we got to The Dalles the prairie began.

Drove through (indistinguishable) from Dalles to Penelton then from Penelton to Lagrand & from Lagrand to Baker & from Baker to Ontario.

Note of Tuesday –

In the prairie look up and see nothing but he gray sky it sure was gray. That is where I was so home sick and sideache.

Wednesday –

Went through 1000 spring. Saw artichen well. In Idaho took a picture at the prairie then a picture of the car in the prairie. Tell more about snow at Twin Falls – worse at American Falls, less at Pocatello. Stayed overnight.

Thursday morning, April 13, 1933

Left Pocatello in the morning at 6:15 a.m. Starting from here with snow and ice in the road as we were going along the 100 miles to drive out of Idaho were terrible ice and snow we sure had to go slow. In Idaho were the snow fields. (St. Marie Hotel at Pocatello)

Wednesday rest of it –

Tell about man going off road in prairie. Idaho – it's almost sickning to see all the dead rabbits on the road in the prairie. We only saw rabbits on the prairie, but so many dead ones.

Wyoming – Thursday

In Wy. The snow quit. It was a wanderfall trip through Idaho & Wyoming. Driving along the Rocky Mts. In Idaho it wasn't so nice because we had to watch the roads so very close on account of the snow. Then in Wy the road was alright. A wanderfall trip in Wyoming.

Thou hast made known to me the ways of life; thou shalt make me full of joy with thy countenance. Acts 2:28

In Wy. We meet in the distance of 5 miles the most sheep a person would want to see. In Wy had a piece of the road that was about as bad as country road – snow, ice, mud & slippery OH! That lasted for 50 miles the all of a sudden we drove on to the pavement ever since. This doesn't give you the chills nothing does. Going through the prairie for 200 mi. not seeing a house, one sheep herder, but every now & then a car. On top of it all thinking of Mabel always singing a cowboy song.

Snow – cold.

Soda Springs, Wy. Put heater on – cold. Through the prairie cold. Drove to Rock River for night. Wy and Ida artificial line. Ore & Ida snake River.

Friday, April 14, 1933
Left R. River at 4:25 a.m. Cold. Drive terrible. Was froze stiff.

Friday – Nebraska
Line at Wyo & Neb artificial. Nebraska wonderful course Western Nebraska& Eastern Wyo about the same after going about 25 minutes into Neb. It starts to come a few houses & Cornfields. Neb & Iowa – corn states. After in Neb. It becomes to feel more pleasant. All the wild ducks swimming in rivers, lakes other streams. Tell how they cut corn. Illinois corn state. Missouri River boundry line between Ill. & Iowa. Dirty river.

Saturday

Nebraska & Iowa. Tell about rest of Neb. Leaving Grand Island at 3:10 a.m. stopped at Blair, Neb. Last city in Neb. Had breakfast – crossed Missouri River a dirty river. Large bridge – pay to cross. In Chicago. Artificial line between Ill & Indiana & Indiana to Michigan. Uncle August lost in Indiana twice.

(When Mildred starts a sentence with "Tell," I believe she is making a note to share this experience with her sister Frances.)

*Columbia River Highway
**Columbia River

www.ingramcontent.com/pod-product-compliance
Lightning Source LLC
Chambersburg PA
CBHW071029280326
41935CB00011B/1504